Dealing With The Past

A Note to Ambassador Haass

From

Desmond Rea & Robin Masefield

Dealing With The Past

ISBN 978-1-909751-11-8

Published by Decision Partnership
The Mount Business & Conference Centre Belfast,
2 Woodstock Link, Belfast, BT6 8DD,
United Kingdom

Preface

"The Panel of Parties in the Northern Ireland Executive is an independently chaired panel created in July 2013. In the May 2013 strategy, *Together, Building a United Community*, the members of the Northern Ireland Executive recognised obstacles that are frustrating the movement to a society based on equality of opportunity, good relations, and reconciliation. In the body of the May strategy, the five Executive Parties proposed a way forward involving the establishment of a Panel of Parties in the Northern Ireland Executive (Panel) to consider parades and protests; flags, symbols and emblems, and related matters; and the past."

The Panel is charged with bringing forward consensus recommendations whenever possible.

The Panel has an independent Chair, Ambassador Richard N. Haass, and Vice-Chair, Meghan L. O'Sullivan.

Professor Sir Desmond Rea, as the first Chair of the Northern Ireland Policing Board and Robin Masefield, as a former senior Northern Ireland Office civil servant and Director General of Prisons have for some years been concerned about how Northern Ireland in dealing with its troubled past could do so and at the same time achieve a healthy balance with the future. We have pleasure in submitting this *Note* to Ambassador Haass and through him to the Panel of Parties.

November/December 2013

Contents

Chapter One
An Intractable Problem?

1.1 The Background

Michael Cassidy, the South African church leader, remarked in October 1996:

> '*One notices how people are gripped by the past, remembering the past, feeding on the past; people are constantly remembering this betrayal or that battle; this plantation or that pogrom; this martyr or this murderer; and those realities of the past feed into the present in Ireland more than anywhere I have been'.* (Quoted in the Report of the Independent Review of Parades and Marches 1997.)

The Northern Ireland Policing Board (the Policing Board or Board), like most organisations, dealt with matters pro-actively and re-actively. In respect of the former category of matters they could be programmed in say a corporate plan or unprogrammed. *Dealing With Northern Ireland's Troubled Past*, whilst unprogrammed, was a preoccupation of the Chairman almost from the beginning of the Policing Board. During the first half of 2003 he spent some time consulting with others and drafting a paper entitled *Seeking To Hold The Past In Healthy Balance with The Future.* Having obtained the endorsement of the Vice-Chairman, Denis Bradley, he sought to initiate a debate at the Board by obtaining the permission of Members of the Board's Corporate Policy Committee to read the paper to them; they agreed. This short book is in larger part about that unfolding debate. Although the paper was never endorsed by the Board, both the Chairman and Vice-Chairman were permitted to speak publicly to it as individual Members. Later the Chief Constable endorsed it.

The next section of this book reminds us of the scale of the deaths and injuries caused during the Troubles. Many of these occurred in incidents that the former Royal Ulster Constabulary (RUC) were very ill-equipped to respond to at the time, in part through the sheer scale of the effort that would have been required to undertake as thorough an investigation into each serious incident as that which would have been undertaken in comparable circumstances in Great Britain or the Republic of Ireland. (It is worth noting that the level of the deaths in Northern Ireland during the Troubles would – had it been repeated in Great Britain – have resulted in well over 100,000 fatalities.)

The other area of interest in this book relates to an initiative taken by Chief

Constable Hugh Orde. He drew up proposals to set up a Serious Crime Review Team, based initially within the Police Service of Northern Ireland (the Police Service or PSNI) that would be resourced to focus solely on reinvestigating previous murders. The team was eventually to be called the Historical Enquiries Team (HET). This was designed to free up the bulk of the PSNI to focus on present and future policing challenges.

Separately, Professor Rea and Mr Bradley sent the paper referred to above to the Secretary of State for Northern Ireland. It would appear that the paper, although the Board were not persuaded by its proposals, played a significant part in shaping the thinking of Secretaries of State for Northern Ireland Paul Murphy and others in setting up the subsequent review jointly led by the Right Reverend Robin Eames, Archbishop of Armagh, and Denis Bradley; their report and its proposals are summarised in this book. As it is recorded in the Welsh Mabinogion – "Let the one who would be the leader be the bridge".

This book can only highlight selectively a number of the particular incidents from the past that had a major bearing on the work of the Policing Board, such as the Omagh and Claudy bombs and the deaths that were considered by Judge Cory in the assessment he undertook at the request of the British and Irish Governments. This is not in any way to belittle or diminish all the other fatalities, and indeed life-changing injuries that impacted so grievously on so many of the people in Northern Ireland during the Troubles. As is made clear in the concluding section of this book, in no way would the authors of this book accept a hierarchy of victims.

1.2 How Many Died/Were Injured?

The *Report of the Consultative Group on the Past* jointly chaired by the former Archbishop of Armagh, the Right Reverend Robin Eames, and Denis Bradley noted that as a result of the conflict between 1969 and 2001:

- 3523 persons were killed.
- of the total killed 2055 (58%) were attributed to Republican paramilitary groups, 1020 (29%) to Loyalist paramilitary groups, 368 (10%) to Security Forces and 80 (2%) to persons unknown.
- The breakdown of those killed was as follows: civilians (1855); members of the Security Forces (1123); Republican paramilitary group members (394) and Loyalist paramilitary group members (151).
- In addition some 47,000 people in Northern Ireland sustained injuries, in 16,200 bombing and 37,000 shooting incidents.

- A total of 19,600 individuals received a sentence of imprisonment for scheduled offences, ie crimes that the legislation determined were related to terrorism.

The Fourteen Most Serious Incidents: in terms of persons killed the authors have looked at 41 incidents, which could be described as "major"- Eames/ Bradley isolate 19 and rightly comment: *'Although no list of some of the worst violent incidents during the Troubles can be other than selective, it may help to frame the context for consideration of the peace process'* and we would add of the challenge of *'dealing with the past'*.

The 14 most 'major' incidents were:

- On 17 May 1974 33 civilians were killed plus possibly 300 injured by the UVF in a series of bomb attacks in Dublin and Monaghan and for which no-one has been charged;
- On 15 August 1998 29 civilians and two unborn babies were killed plus over 200 injured in the Omagh bombing by RIRA and for which two persons were charged, one convicted and later quashed;
- On 21 November 1974 21 civilians were killed plus 182 injured in IRA bomb attacks in Birmingham city centre, for which six persons were charged and six convicted and later quashed;
- On 27 August 1979 19 persons (18 soldiers and one civilian) were killed at Narrow Water. The soldiers killed were killed by the IRA and the civilian by the Army in subsequent gunfire, plus eight injured and for which no-one has been charged;
- On 6 December 1982 17 persons (11 soldiers and six civilians) were killed and 30 injured by an INLA bomb at the Droppin' Well bar, Ballykelly and for which five persons were charged and five convicted;
- On 4 December 1971 15 civilians were killed plus 16 injured in the bombing of McGurk's Bar by the UVF, for which one person was charged and one convicted.
- On 30 January 1972 (Bloody Sunday) 14 civilians were killed and 13 injured by the Army during a civil rights march in Derry and for which no-one has been charged;
- On 17 February 1978 12 persons (11 civilians and one member of the security services) were killed plus 23 injured in an IRA firebomb attack

at the La Mon Hotel for which two were charged and one convicted.

- On 8 November 1987 12 civilians were killed plus 68 injured in an IRA bomb attack at the Remembrance Day service in Enniskillen, and for which no-one has been charged;
- On 4 February 1974 nine soldiers and three civilians were killed and 38 injured in an IRA bomb attack on the M62 in Yorkshire and for which one person was charged, one convicted and later quashed.
- On 5 January 1976 ten civilians were shot dead and one person injured by the IRA at Kingsmill, Armagh, and for which no-one has been charged;
- On 23 October 1993 nine civilians and one member of the IRA were killed and 58 injured when an IRA bomb exploded prematurely on the Shankill Road, Belfast, and for which one person was charged and one convicted.
- On 21 July 1972 seven civilians and two soldiers were killed and possibly 130 overall injured at Oxford Street Bus Station and the Cavehill Road during the 19 bomb attacks on 'Bloody Friday' and for which three were charged and two convicted;
- On 31 July 1972 nine civilians were killed and 31 injured in an IRA bomb attack in Claudy village and for which no-one has been charged.

In total as a result of these 14 major incidents 222 persons were killed. In respect of the 27 remaining incidents three led to nine deaths each, four to eight deaths each, one to seven deaths, seven to six deaths each and 12 to five deaths each. 168 in all, giving a total for the 41 incidents of 390 deaths.

Of the 41 major incidents:

- Republicans perpetrated 28 and killed 267, of whom 170 were civilians;
- Loyalists perpetrated ten and killed 94 and all but two were civilians;
- the Army in two incidents killed 23, of whom 15 were civilians; and
- one incident in which six civilians were killed was considered perpetrated by Loyalists.

1.3 Re-tracing Our (Political) Steps

Let us re-trace our steps: by July 2001 the IRA had not decommissioned and David Trimble resigned as First Minister. Dixon and O'Kane record:

'that the two governments tried to re-launch the 'peace process' with a 'final', 'non-negotiable' plan, which was published in August 2001 after intense all-party talks at Weston Park in mid-July. The proposals sought to appeal to republicans by promising demilitarisation, new police legislation to reflect more fully the Patten Report, an international judge [Cory] *to investigate controversial killings* [Patrick Finucane, Robert Hamill, Rosemary Nelson and Billy Wright in Northern Ireland and Chief Superintendent Breen and Superintendent Buchanan and Lord Justice and Lady Gibson], *the demolition of British security bases and an undertaking not to pursue on-the-runs (people wanted for offences committed before the IRA called its ceasefire). The proposals argued that decommissioning was indispensable.'*

The Foreword to each of the four 'Cory Collusion Inquiry Reports' is the same. It reads:

'I was asked by the Government of the United Kingdom to investigate allegations of collusion by members of the security forces in the context of the deaths of Patrick Finucane, Robert Hamill, Rosemary Nelson and Billy Wright and to report with recommendations for any further action. These four reports are the product of my investigation.

It is important that I should make clear what I have taken my task to involve. My task was not to make final determinations of fact or attributions of responsibility. I had the preliminary role of assessing whether there is a case to be answered as to possible collusion, in a wide sense, by members of the security forces in these deaths such as to warrant further and more detailed inquiry. It necessarily follows from this role that

my findings are provisional only, and cannot be taken to be final determinations of any matter. It is right that this point should be emphasised at the outset, in fairness to the individuals referred to in the reports.

The nature of the task which I undertook was reflected in the nature of my investigation in each case. My investigations took the straightforward form of scrutiny of the documentary evidence which exists in relation to each of these cases. Given the preliminary and provisional nature of the task assigned to me, and the desirability of arriving at recommendations expeditiously, it was not necessary or appropriate for me to hear any oral evidence from the individuals referred to in my reports. Obviously, before any final findings of fact or determinations of responsibility could be made, it would be necessary for individuals to have an opportunity of answering any potential criticisms which might be made of them.

For the reasons which I have given in my reports, I have found that in each of the four cases the documentary evidence indicates that there are matters of concern which would warrant further and more detailed inquiry.'

For Robert Hamill, Rosemary Nelson and Billy Wright the further and more detailed inquiries were to be in public. For Patrick Finucane the inquiry deemed necessary by the family has still to take place.

1.4 The Omagh Bombing:

On 12 December 2001 the Police Ombudsman for Northern Ireland presented to the Northern Ireland Policing Board,'*... a highly critical report on the policing investigation of the Omagh bombing. The report was in turn strongly criticised by the Chief Constable.'*

On 7 February 2002 the Board issued its considered response to the Ombudsman's report and in particular to its recommendations. At its third meeting held on 12 December 2001 the Board agreed to meet not only with the Police Ombudsman and the Chief Constable but also with the victims of the Omagh bombing to discuss the report and the Chief Constable's response. The Chief Constable met with the victims of the Omagh bombing on 24 January 2002 and accompanied by Board Members and local MLA, Joe Byrne, the Board's Corporate Policy Committee met with them on 28 January 2002. (NB over the Christmas period the Chairman and Vice-Chairman of the Board made contact with the following persons from Omagh: Michael Gallagher, Chair, Omagh Relatives Group; Rev. Robert Herron, local Presbyterian Minister; Father Kevin Mullan, local Catholic priest; and David Bolton, Trauma Centre.) At the 28 January 2002 meeting with the representatives of the victims (dead and injured) their pain was palpable and unforgettable, as it was with victims of other atrocities and of individual incidents regardless of origin. As the years have passed the victims of Omagh faced with the lack of criminal convictions for the Omagh bombing turned beyond that successfully to the civil courts. On 21 March 2013 the *Irish Times* reported that *'[on the balance of probabilities] two dissident republicans Colm Murphy and Seamus Daly were held responsible for the 1998 Real IRA Omagh bombing and along with two other republicans [Michael McKevitt and Liam Campbell] are now liable to pay £1.6m in compensation to a number of Omagh families'.* (NB While the four dissidents were previously held liable in a 2009 civil case, Murphy and Daly won a retrial in a 2011 appeal.) Mr Justice Gillen in his civil case judgment found the case against them *'overwhelming'*. He declared in court,

> *'The barrier of time has not served to disguise the enormity of this crime, the wickedness of its perpetrators, and the grief of those who must bear the consequences. Even 15 years on nothing can dilute the pulsing horror of what happened.'*

1.5 The Claudy Bombing

On 19 December 2002 Assistant Chief Constable Sam Kinkaid informed the Board that in August 2002 he had *'directed … that a senior detective review the investigation into (the 14th major incident listed above viz) the Claudy bombing,'* that he would be briefing the injured and the relatives of those who died the following day, and be attaching a copy of the following statement released to the press on 20 December 2002:

> *'I have just briefed the injured and the relatives of those killed at Claudy on 31 July 1972, on the initial findings of the review into the investigation.*
>
> *Three bombs were planted in Claudy. They exploded killing nine people. Over 30 people were injured. Claudy remains one of the worst unsolved atrocities of the Troubles.*
>
> *I commissioned the review in August 2002 following the 30th anniversary of the bombing. The review is being carried out by a Senior Detective attached to North Region of the Police Service of Northern Ireland. He reports directly to me. The purpose of the review is to see if there are any new or existing lines of enquiry that the PSNI can take forward.*
>
> *I later amended the terms of reference for the review to include an assessment of a letter purporting to come from a "Father Liam". This spoke of the involvement of a Catholic priest in the bomb attack. The text of the letter does raise a number of questions as to whether or not it was written by a person who knew the priest in question. The forensic examination of the letter has not yet been completed.*

In a search of 1972 papers, information has been found which clearly indicates that a parish priest in the South Derry area was a member of the Provisional IRA and was actively involved in terrorism. Intelligence also indicates that he was involved in the Claudy bomb. Records show he provided an alibi for a person suspected of playing a prominent role in the atrocity. This priest is now deceased. We do not intend to publicly identify the priest or any other suspect in the Claudy incident. Such matters will remain confidential.

An examination of the 1972 and later material has given the review team some understanding of those suspected of involvement in the bomb attack, the part they played and why so many people died at Claudy. We have also tried to discover why no-one has been charged. Our investigations required us to approach both Church authorities and the Government to ask for sight of documents. We are grateful for the assistance given to date.

Our enquiries have revealed that a member of the public briefed the then Cardinal and a senior police officer on the role of the priest not long after the date of the bombing. We have also discovered papers indicating that in late November 1972 the police briefed NIO officials on some of the priest's alleged activities.

In addition, papers were found relating to a discussion held on 5 December 1972 between the Secretary of State at the time, William Whitelaw, and Cardinal Conway. This private discussion occurred at one of the regular meetings that they held to address issues relating to the Troubles. On 6 December 1972, the day after the meeting, a briefing letter was sent from a senior NIO official to Police Headquarters indicating that the private matter discussed related to the activities of the priest.

That letter of 6 December 1972 indicates that the Secretary of State gave the Cardinal a full account of his disgust at the priest's behaviour and also indicates that the Cardinal knew that the priest was behaving improperly. The letter then states that the Cardinal mentioned the possibility of transferring the priest to Donegal. By January 1973 police reports show that the priest was not being seen in the South Derry area. Intelligence suggested he was working in Donegal. Police cannot find any record that the priest was ever arrested or interviewed about his alleged involvement in the Claudy bombing, or any other terrorist offence.

As the army had primacy in relation to security activities at that time, the PSNI has written to them, the NIO, and the Catholic Church requesting sight of any additional papers in relation to the Claudy bombing, the role of the priest, and subsequent events. This is very much an interim report to the families and they will be briefed on further developments.

There has been some media speculation that the then Bishop of Derry was involved in 1972 in matters relating to the priest. Police have not discovered any evidence of this.

It is clear that the relatives of those who died in the bomb attack on Claudy village and those who were injured have not obtained justice. I regret this very much and in particular that opportunities to arrest and interview all of the suspects were not taken in 1972. I have told the families that my officers are fully committed to doing everything possible to bring those responsible before the courts. We would therefore appeal to anyone who has information that could assist the police to contact the detectives at Strand Road police station.'

Again on Friday, 20 December 2002, and on the back of a most helpful note prepared by officials of the Board, the Chairman issued on behalf of the Board the following press release which in larger part he drafted:

'The Claudy bombing on 31 July 1972, which claimed the lives of nine people and injured over 30 was an appalling atrocity and the investigation which followed left many questions unanswered. In August this year, 30 years after the bombing, the PSNI initiated a review into the original investigation.

I have now received details of the initial findings from the PSNI review and have passed this information on to all members of the Northern Ireland Policing Board.

Whilst the bombing took place over 30 years ago I fully appreciate that the grief of the relatives today, particularly in light of the PSNI findings, will be intense. I recognise that given the information they have received, the families of the victims of the bombing will no doubt be feeling many emotions including bewilderment, hurt and anger.

The Policing Board has responsibility for ensuring that the police service is effective, efficient and impartial. It is also important that the police has the confidence of the community it serves. With that in mind I welcome the frankness of the PSNI statement.

Given that the Board's key function is to hold the PSNI to account I expect it will take the earliest opportunity it has to question the Chief Constable and Assistant Chief Constable Kinkaid further about this matter. It is clear from what has come to light today that people will need reassurance. The Policing Board is an essential contributor to achieving that confidence.

I welcome the commitment given to the families by the Assistant Chief Constable today that the PSNI will do everything possible to bring those responsible for the Claudy bombing before the courts.

There is no doubt that the events of 31 July, and in particular the subsequent discussions which took place in November and December 1972 raise serious concerns. I can assure the whole community that the Policing Board will do everything within its remit to ensure that public concerns are fully addressed.'

At the 11th *public session* of the Board held on 6 February 2003 the following question was put to ACC Kinkaid by *Independent Member* Brian Dougherty*:*

> *"Chief Constable, would you please comment on the current position regarding the police investigation into the Claudy bombing and provide assurances that the families of the victims and the people of Claudy themselves will get the recognition, respect, equality and ultimate closure that they deserve?"*

ACC Kinkaid replied

> *'Chairman, the ongoing enquiry is a review of the original investigation. At the conclusion of the review, the reviewing officer will bring forward recommendations to myself and the Chief Constable as to whether there is any prospect of advancing the investigation towards criminal charges. 23 next of kin of the deceased have been identified, together with 20 surviving injured and all these people have had contact with the Family Liaison Officer who has been dealing with them.*
>
> *Currently the review team is speaking to many retired officers who were involved in the original investigation and re-examining issues relating to intelligence and forensics. It is anticipated that all material*

will hopefully be reviewed in about three months, at which time the reviewing officer will prepare a report. But it should be noted that this timescale might change, should the review team discover other issues of note that they feel they are going to have to examine.

I can give a full assurance that the families of those who were injured will be given full support by the PSNI. They are being kept informed.'

In response to a question at the Policing Board meeting held on 6 November 2003 ACC Kinkaid, now ACC Crime, updated Members regarding the review into the Claudy bomb investigation. The Board noted that the investigation was on-going and families had also been updated by the PSNI.

At the Board meeting held on 7 April 2005 the Board asked for and received in the *public session* an update on the ongoing investigation into the Claudy bombing. ACC Kinkaid concluded his reply as follows:

'As we have done in some of the recent murder investigations, I am happy at a further date, to come with the Senior Investigating Officer to a private session of the Board and to brief members on progress to date.'

Jumping a few years – on 13 October 2010, Detective Chief Superintendent Tom Hanley, Head of PSNI's Serious Crime Branch, wrote to the Policing Board regarding *'the investigation into the Claudy bombing in 1972'* as follows:

'As Head of the PSNI's Serious Crime Branch my operational responsibilities include managing the effective investigation of murders which have occurred in Northern Ireland.

The Claudy investigation has recently been transferred from the Historic Enquiries Team (HET) to Serious Crime Branch. The scale and complexity of this investigation can best be progressed by Serious Crime Branch, who have the necessary resources available to conduct such an enquiry.

I have appointed a team of Detectives to conduct an initial case assessment on my behalf. When this is completed I will dedicate a Senior Investigating Officer and a Major Investigation Team to progress the investigation.

At this stage it is unclear if the victims wish to be treated as a united victims group or as individual families. I have written to the victim's commissioner in an effort to shed some light on this matter. I have enclosed a copy letter which has been sent to each of the families.

Detective Sergeant Hugh McDonogh, PSNI Ladas Drive, who is a trained Family Liaison Coordinator, will be available to the families to assist with any immediate concerns they may have.'

The helpful note prepared by officials of the Board on 20 December 2002 and referred to above put the Claudy bombing in the context of 1972: it was one of a catalogue of incidents (see list above). 1972 saw an escalation of the IRA campaign and Loyalist activities, the Army's Operation Motorman to clear Northern Ireland's towns and cities of 'no-go' areas and intense political change. In respect of the latter at the end of October 1972 the UK Government published a discussion document entitled 'The Future of Northern Ireland' which included devolution and an 'Irish dimension'.

1.6 'On-The-Runs'

On the back of the Police Ombudsman's recommendations as contained in her *'Report on the Investigation of Matters Relating to the Omagh Bombing of 15 August 1998'* the Policing Board agreed that HMIC David Blakey oversee *'The Review of Terrorist Linked Murder Inquiries'*; the eventual title of his report was *'A Report on Murder Investigation for the Chief Constable of the Police Service of Northern Ireland, 2003'*. HMI Blakey commented on 'On-the-Runs' as follows:

'A complex and highly sensitive overlapping issue concerns those people identified as being 'On the Run'. These are people, believed to be 'wanted' for terrorist related crimes, including murder. The Good Friday Agreement led to the release from prison of convicted terrorists. It did not however provide amnesty for unconvicted terrorists and this remains a highly sensitive, political and moral dilemma. The PSNI continues to wrestle with uncertainty in these areas. In terms of investigating the huge number of outstanding archived murders (outlined earlier) and those persons considered to be 'On the Run', HMIC believes, in order to enable the service to focus on identified priorities, that PSNI urgently requires clear guidance from the highest levels.'

Chapter Two
The Past Versus the Future

2.1 Initiating The Debate

At the Policing Board's Corporate Policy Committee meeting held on 17 June 2003 the Chairman sought and received the permission of Members of the Board to read to them a paper entitled *'Seeking to hold the Past in a Healthy Balance with the Future'*. He had written the paper in the context of (a) the numbers killed and injured in the Troubles and in particular in the 14 major incidents listed referred to above, in which special mention was made of the Omagh and Claudy bombings; (b) the Chief Constable's estimate of *'2,000 plus unsolved killings'*; (c) the Cory Reports and recommendations and (d) the need to make political progress. He had discussed the paper with the Board's Vice-Chairman and received his endorsement of it. The paper read as follows:

'Seeking to Hold the Past in Healthy Balance with the Future

1. ***Introduction***

David Bolton in a recent article posed the following question:

"to what degree is progress dependent on addressing the past?"

Which he answered as follows:

"I am reminded of John Paul Lederach's dictum:

> *'remember and change where the past is held in healthy balance with the future'*

and how people should remember in helpful and creative ways while engaging in positive change. We can either sweep the past under the carpet or engage in endless and divisive forensic purity. A man whose daughter died in the Oklahoma bombing comes to mind. He reached a pivotal moment in his grief when he enquired of himself:

> *"what would it take to enable me to be reconciled to his loss and to inhabit the future, for his own personal peace of mind, and for our collective good we need to ask ourselves the same question ... and thereafter agree on a 'good enough' way of settling the past."*

It would seem a sensible approach:

- *to learn from the past in a positive way;*
- *to understand the present; and*
- *to provide for the future in such a way that we do not regress to the past.*

2. ***Context***

In the Troubles some 3,366 people have been killed, of those 1,525 were Catholics and 1,250 Protestants. 300 police officers were killed, and 9,000 police officers were injured, as were 46,753 lay people.

Many to this day mourn their dead. Many to this day are bruised and hurt. Too many cases are unresolved – some 1,800 – and relatives left without closure. Some families believe, rightly or wrongly, that the killing of their relatives involved collusion with the security forces and want public inquiries.

There have been two processes running concurrently which have sought to address the Northern Ireland conflict:

- *first,* ***the peace process****; and*
- *secondly.* ***the political process*** *(Note : The parameters of the latter are well known and are not the purport of this chapter).*

Sinn Fein has argued that their paramilitary wing, namely PIRA

  - *was an army; and*
  - *was engaged in a war; and*
  - *since it was a war the prisoners of war should be released.*

By releasing the prisoners does this not mean that the British Government has implicitly recognised Sinn Fein's argument?

Let us envisage, what we all hope is a possible scenario: election in November. This is likely to lead to a cross party Executive including Sinn Fein.

In June 2002 Peter Cory QC was appointed. His Terms of Reference were as follows:

> *"to conduct a thorough investigation into allegations of collusion by the security forces in six particular cases to which the two Governments committed themselves following the discussions with the Northern Ireland parties at Weston Park last summer."*

Among other things his letter of appointment states:

> *"in the event that a Public Inquiry is recommended, the relevant Government will implement that recommendation."*

Assume when he reports that he recommends one or more inquiries, which in turn lead to cases against police officers, either former or present, being referred to the Director of Public Prosecutions. We could, therefore, have on the one hand a former alleged paramilitary sitting as a Minister, and policemen in the dock.

That situation will create for this society and this Policing Board a number of critical issues:

- *an even more divided society than we have at present;*
- *police time being consumed on investigations going back into the not so recent past; and*
- *a deterioration in police morale.*

3. ***Alternatives***

3.1 *Article 2 of the European Convention on Human Rights states that "everyone's right to life shall be protected by the law". On that basis collusion and misdemeanours by the State must never happen and the perpetrators must be pursued through public inquiry to prosecutions; or*

3.2 *As of, say the signing of the Joint Declaration, 'the slate should be wiped clean and as a society we should look to the future'; or*

3.3 *Accept that in a war nasty things happen on both sides. While you can argue that more can be expected of a State, it would seem disingenuous to do so if, as Sinn Fein has argued, and the argument appears to have been implicitly accepted, that they were engaged in a war, and not in terrorism ... a middle way involving:*

3.3.1 the release of the prisoners should now be extended to an amnesty for <u>all</u>;

3.3.2 there should be no more inquiries;

3.3.3 a Truth Commission should be established immediately:

- *People could begin voluntarily to tell their stories.*
- *When the main paramilitary organisations agree to go to the Truth Commission, the United Kingdom Government should agree to do so too.*

The Chairman, having read the paper to Members, concluded by adding that, if Northern Ireland did not face up to dealing with its past in a constructive and imaginative manner, there were consequences: three of which were referred to above. Each Member of the Committee expressed his/her view in a wide ranging discussion, which covered among other matters the following:

- the financial and legal consequences of investigating 1,800 unsolved murders;
- the need for an elective commission on the past;
- public inquiries;
- truth commissions; and
- resources needed to police the past, the present and the future.

The Committee agreed that a discussion paper should be put to a future Board meeting.

At the Board meeting held on 3 March 2004 the Board discussed a radio interview which the Chairman had given to the BBC regarding the contents of his paper on *Dealing With The Past.* The Board recognised that the Chairman had presented a short paper on the subject at an earlier meeting and that at that meeting there had not been any objections to a proposal that the issues discussed in the paper be discussed more widely provided the Chairman emphasised that he was speaking in a personal capacity; it was noted that the Chairman in the interview had done so. During the interview the Chairman, when asked for his own approach, argued for 3.3 down to and including 3.3.2 of the above paper. A number of Members commended the Chairman for raising the issues. It was agreed that a copy of the paper referred to during the interview be circulated to all Members.

2.2 Westminster's Own Inquiry

The Policing Board at its meeting on 1 December 2004 noted the following press release, which had been issued by the Westminster Parliament's Northern Ireland Affairs Committee (NIAC) on 4 November 2004:

'NEW INQUIRY: RECONCILIATION – WAYS OF DEALING WITH NORTHERN IRELAND'S PAST

The Committee has decided to conduct an inquiry into possible ways of dealing with Northern Ireland's past. It therefore proposes to examine:

The experience of efforts in other jurisdictions to move forward from a history of division and conflict, on a basis as widely acceptable as possible to affected communities and individuals who have suffered from violence.

The Committee may also choose to examine associated issues which arise in the course of the inquiry.

The Rt Hon Michael Mates MP, Chairman of the Committee, explained the intention of the Committee:

"In May the Secretary of State for Northern Ireland announced that he was embarking on a programme of discussions about how Northern Ireland could find 'ways of dealing with the past which recognises the pain, grief and anger associated with it' but which 'enables it to build a better future for the next generation'. The Committee wholeheartedly welcomes this initiative.

"The purpose of the inquiry we have announced today is to seek out and illuminate ways which have been used to help resolve similar conflicts elsewhere, and which could assist the process of healing society in Northern Ireland. Our intention is not to arrive at a narrow and prescriptive set of recommendations. Rather, by illuminating approaches which have had success elsewhere, we hope to make a positive contribution to the desire of the overwhelming majority of the people of Northern Ireland to seek ways of easing the hurt of the last 30 years."

The Board also noted that the NIAC had invited individuals or organisations with an interest in this matter to submit written evidence not later than 3 December 2004. On 20 January 2005 there was a follow-up press release from the NIAC asking *'that those who have not yet [responded] to the initial announcement and who wish to contribute to write to us.'*

The Board discussed the submission of a paper prepared previously by the Chairman and endorsed by the Vice-Chairman entitled *'Seeking to Hold the Past in a Healthy Balance with the Future'*. Members indicated that they were content for both to submit the paper to the NIAC in personal capacities. The minute of the 1 December 2004 meeting adds:

> *'Whilst members agreed that the general debate on the issue of dealing with Northern Ireland's past should be driven by others outside the policing environment, members also agreed that there was a need for further debate within the Board.'*

In a draft prepared for a proposed submission by the Policing Board and before the above decision, paragraphs on *'the policing context'* and *'the way forward'* took the Chief Constable's and the Chairman's and Vice-Chairman's thinking forward ...

> ***'The Policing Context***
>
> *Within the new policing arrangements there is an overwhelming desire to move forward and police the future. That is not to say that past unresolved cases are not worthy of police time and effort.*
>
> *There is a desire to work within the current legislative framework and the European Convention on Human Rights (ECHR) context and a desire for justice but from a practical perspective Patten's 7,500 officers did not take account of a need to police the past to the extent that is now becoming evident and indeed being demanded from some quarters.*
>
> *The potential for many re-investigations (Cory, through Police Ombudsman for Northern Ireland cases, 1,900 unsolved murders, the pressure on the Chief Constable to investigate the murders of policemen and women) has obvious resource implications in an area (investigations) that the Police Service of Northern Ireland (PSNI) already has a shortage.*
>
> *The PSNI's Chief Constable has weighed this balance, and in policing terms found a positive way forward. He has secured support from the NIO to put in place a dedicated unit of detectives to apply modern investigative techniques to review every one of these outstanding unsolved murder cases. Through this review process, those cases can be identified in which there is realistic potential for the crime to be solved, and this smaller number of cases can then be more thoroughly investigated.*

The question has to be asked though, is the desire for justice within the gift of PSNI to deliver – what do the families of the victims want?

Way Forward

There are many options for ways forward, and it is helpful that the Northern Ireland Affairs Committee has turned its attention to this important issue. The Policing Board, in this paper, does not seek either to rehearse those options, or to recommend one particular route.

Whatever option is ultimately chosen, ownership of that choice across our society is of fundamental importance.

Instead, we put forward for consideration the idea that the British Government, in consultation with the Irish Government, assumes, and begins to discharge, their rightful duty, and to immediately establish a Cross-Community Body which would:

- *deliberate on the past;*
- *consult with the Northern Ireland community and*
- *make proposals to Government as to a more constructive way forward in dealing with the past.*

We propose this in the belief that it is necessary first to seek consensus on the structure of a way forward rather than simply introducing one of the oft-rehearsed mechanisms. Although there may already be a wide consensus on the need to address the past to help heal society and move towards a shared vision of a prosperous, inclusive and peaceful future, work needs first to be done on getting everybody on board. By so doing … this is the best way of holding the past in a healthy balance with the future.'

At the meeting of the Policing Board held on 3 February 2005 the Chairman referred to a discussion at the previous meeting and to the consensus among Members that there was need for further discussion within the Board on the issue of '*dealing with the past*'. A motion was proposed, seconded and unanimously agreed that a group of Members should consider the issue. It was further agreed:

- that a representative of the PSNI should brief Members on the investigation of historic cases; and
- that a representative of the Northern Ireland Office (NIO) should brief Members on the Northern Ireland Secretary of State's views on the issue of dealing with the past, including victims.

At the Policing Board meeting of 7 April 2005 Members' attention was drawn to two press releases made by Secretary of State, Paul Murphy. In the first, dated 1 March 2005, he announced proposals for a Victims and Survivors Commissioner as part of a detailed consultation on the future of services for victims and survivors of the Troubles.

'The Troubles have left their mark on the people of Northern Ireland and all those affected by the conflict. And the human cost extends beyond these victims, to their families and friends, to all those who survived their ordeals, and to the wider community which struggles still to heal the divisions that were created and became entrenched.

The pain of loss is still keenly felt by those who lost loved ones. The Government cannot hope to change that. But there is a sense in which we in Northern Ireland need to come to terms with what has happened over the past 35 years: to tackle the legacy in a way that respects the suffering and loss that has been experienced; but which also allows the community as a whole to build a future that is not overshadowed by the events of the past.

Last spring, the Prime Minister said that he hoped that the Government could find a way to deal with Northern Ireland's past. Since then I have been reflecting on how we might begin this process.

My view remains that Northern Ireland needs its own tailored approach to dealing with the past. That is not to say that we cannot learn from the experiences of other societies that have faced a difficult and turbulent period in their recent history. But any process for dealing with Northern Ireland's past will require an approach that acknowledges and respects its unique features as well as its similarities to situations elsewhere.

I also believe that the scope and aims of any process need to be widely understood and agreed, and must be capable of commanding support and credibility right across the community. Government has the ultimate responsibility for ensuring that an appropriate mechanism is found for dealing with the past to the satisfaction of all sections of the community. But I recognise too that, for some, the Government's role in past events is itself seen as an issue; and it is hard for some sections of the community to see us as a genuinely neutral party. Neither does the Government have a monopoly on wisdom, and I recognise the major contribution that many practitioners and other bodies are already making in this field.

These considerations have led me to conclude that any process for dealing with the past in Northern Ireland cannot be designed in isolation, or imposed by Government. There will need to be broadly-based consultation that allows individuals and groups across the community to put their views on what form any process might take. And that consultation process itself will need broad cross-community support if the ideas it generates are to be constructively received.

In the light of recent events, I am clear that now is not the right moment to launch such a broadly-based consultation process. And I think that we need to be realistic about what can be achieved in advance of a political settlement. But that is not to say that nothing can be done or that political considerations should forever stand in the way of meaningful progress. There are important steps that the Government can take now to address issues that are at the heart of how we can all deal with Northern Ireland's difficult legacy.

I am therefore announcing today that the Government intends to put in place a new Victims' and Survivors' Commissioner. I believe that this is necessary both to ensure a real focus on the needs of victims and survivors of the Troubles in Northern Ireland and to ensure that their voices continue to be heard and respected. So I am publishing alongside this announcement a consultation paper on the future of victims' and survivors' services for those victims, which includes the Government's initial proposals for the Commissioner's detailed remit. The document sets out proposals for a comprehensive approach to the provision of services, with the Commissioner playing a pivotal role in ensuring effective service delivery and in promoting the interests of all those who have suffered as a result of Northern Ireland's troubled past. One of the Commissioner's responsibilities will be to take forward the establishment of the Victims' and Survivors' Forum envisaged in the Joint Declaration to represent their views in a structured way. That consultation will continue until the end of June this year.

For many victims and survivors, the possibility of coming to terms with what has happened in the past is made more remote because there remain significant unanswered questions, for example about the fate of their loved ones. For many families, the difficulty of not knowing certain details surrounding their loved one's death continues to be a significant issue many years on. The Government recognises that there is a need to address in a systematic way all of the unresolved deaths in Northern Ireland's recent troubled past. As I announced last September, I have been in discussions with the Chief Constable about how the ground-breaking work of the Serious Crime Review Team (SCRT) within the Police Service of Northern Ireland might be expanded to help meet this need. I hope that both we and the PSNI will soon be in a position to say more about the next steps on this. ...'

Subsequently, on 2 June 2008, a Commission for Victims and Survivors was created under the Victims and Survivors (NI) Order 2006, enacted by the Northern Ireland Assembly on 27 May 2008. Four Commissioners were appointed – Patricia MacBride, Mike Nesbitt, Brendan McAllister and Bertha McDougall OBE – on 2 June 2008, for one term of four years.

The principal aim of the Commission is to promote the interests of victims and survivors of the conflict. The Commission has the following six statutory duties:

- to promote awareness of matters relating to the interests of victims and survivors and the need to safeguard those interests;
- to keep under review the adequacy and effectiveness of law and practice affecting the interests of victims and survivors;
- to keep under review the adequacy and effectiveness of services provided for victims and survivors;
- to provide advice to government on matters affecting victims and survivors;
- to ensure that the views of victims and survivors are sought by the Commission in carrying out its work; and
- to make arrangements for a forum for consultation with victims and survivors.

The Commission has the power to conduct research or educational activities and issue guidance on best practice in relation to any matter concerning the interests of victims and survivors.

The Commission may also make representations or recommendations to any body or person concerning the interests of victim and survivors.

The NIAC published its report *'Ways of Dealing with Northern Ireland's Past: Interim Report – Victims and Survivors'* on 8 April 2005. The report urged the UK Government to increase the support it provided to victims and survivors; highlighted the ways in which victims and survivors are at the centre of efforts to build a better future in Northern Ireland; and, while fully supportive of a consultation on the terms of a formal truth recovery process, concluded that the time for this was not yet right. The NIAC in its *'Conclusion – Ways Forward'* stated:

> *'69. There may come a time when a formal, national 'truth recovery' process will contribute positively to the normalisation of society in Northern Ireland but, on the basis of the evidence we have received to date, that time has not yet arrived: the peace is as yet too fragile, the*

scars of the conflict too fresh, the co-operation of parts of Northern Ireland's population is not assured, the political conditions are not yet sufficiently settled, and the conflict in the estimation of many people is not yet finally over. Were such a process to be put in train now, it is our view that this might have the effect of exacerbating community tensions.

70. While we agree, therefore, with the Secretary of State's decision, announced on 1 March, not to proceed at present with his broad consultation on the form of any such process, it will be absolutely essential for the government to ensure that the people of Northern Ireland understand fully that this decision does not imply that the government has ceased to listen to their views on Northern Ireland's future. The government needs also to be constantly alert to, and be prepared actively to nurture, any emerging future consensus which indicates that a formal 'truth recovery' process would be timely and helpful. The Secretary of State has given his personal view on the matter, namely, the hope that such a process will be possible at some suitable time. We agree with that.

71. Properly approached, we consider that the level and quality of support available to victims and survivors, and their status within society is an excellent measure of that society's maturity and sensitivity. We have suggested in this short report that the government needs to examine whether it is giving sufficient priority, and being sufficiently imaginative, in approaching this vital task.

72. Victims represent more than a group which requires and is wholly worthy of broad support. Victims are a primary resource in the process of transformational healing which is at the core of building a better future for Northern Ireland, but their full potential will be unlocked only when their experiences are fully acknowledged and respected throughout Northern Ireland society. Nothing could be more detrimental to the progress of peace and reconciliation in Northern Ireland than to marginalise victims. We look to the government to take a strong lead in ensuring that victims have the influence and esteem, and the part in the rebuilding of society at all levels in Northern Ireland, to which their experiences entitle them.

73. It is far from our intention to place any additional pressures upon those who have suffered most from the 'Troubles'. It is our hope, rather, that the government will do everything possible to enable and empower those who have been touched uniquely by the conflict in order that they may contribute centrally to the wider process of building a normal society for Northern Ireland, should they so wish.

74. While much of the evidence we heard and read has been harrowing, our final impression is one of enormous optimism. There is evidently a keen hunger for peace and the re-creation of mutual respect between the communities, coupled to an ingenuity and imagination on the part of many in seeking a meaning for the future of life in Northern Ireland free from the terror, pain and seeming despair of the past. These admirable characteristics are exemplified magnificently in the lives and experiences of many of those whom we have been privileged to hear from over the past eight weeks. We commend this signal bravery to the government, churches, political parties, and other leaders of civil society as a spur to their own efforts to forge a society for Northern Ireland based firmly on peace and tolerance.'

At the meeting of the Board's Corporate Policy Committee held on 21 April 2005 the Committee agreed:

- that a response to the NIAC's report on *'Ways of dealing with Northern Ireland's Past'* should be considered by the Committee at a future meeting; and
- that questions should be drafted to ask the Chief Constable at the next Board meeting regarding the PSNI's responses to the NIAC reports on *'Dealing with the Past'* and *'Hate Crime in Northern Ireland'*.

At the *private session* of the Policing Board under Corporate Policy Committee business held on 2 June 2005, the Board considered a paper, which highlighted issues identified in NIAC's *'Ways of Dealing with Northern Ireland's Past: Interim Report – Victims and Survivors'* of 8 April 2005. Attached to the paper were the conclusions and recommendations of the Interim Report. The paper highlighted the following issues:

- *'The need for inter-community healing to continue and to receive appropriate recognition, encouragement and financial support.*
- *The need for the pursuit (through a positive political context) of the conditions which will allow peace, and consequently healing, to flourish.*
- *The apparent lack of focus by political parties on the need to fully reflect the desire of ordinary people in Northern Ireland for permanent peace and a normal political process and the imperative for all, including political parties, to engage in a healing process.*

- *The need for any inter or intra healing process to commence when the time is right for victims to be involved in it and similarly the need for all sections of the population to be part of it.*
- *The need for authorities (including PSNI) to consider the level of support given to vulnerable communities and to improve interface with victims and families of victims of crime.*
- *The need for Government to keep the possibility of a truth recovery process under constant review and to be imaginative in their approach to the potential options.*
- *The need for continuing work to improve inter-community relations until the time is right for a 'healing process' [they highlight the potential for such a process to take decades to realistically bring to a conclusion].*
- *The need for the financial compensation received by 'early' victims of the Troubles to be enhanced.*
- *The need for a renewed effort to help the families of the disappeared achieve closure for their hurt.*
- *The differing expectations of those affected by the Troubles varying from the need for a simple acknowledgement, to an apology, to acts of contrition.*
- *The differing views among victims on the benefit of a Victims Commissioner and how this could be mitigated (sufficient remit/powers etc).'*

At the *public session* of the Policing Board held on 2 June 2005 Mr Brian Dougherty, *Independent Member*, asked the Chief Constable:

> *'Would you please comment on two recommendations in the NIAC 'Report on Ways of Dealing with Northern Ireland's Past: Interim Report – Victims and Survivors' viz that relating to the level of support currently afforded to all vulnerable communities and that relating to the way in which the police communicate with victims and their families?'*

The Chief Constable replied as follows:

> *'The critical part of the work at the Historical Enquiries Team will be how we deal with the families and how we liaise with victims' families whilst we reopen and reinvestigate these cases to see if we can take them forward, or where we cannot take them forward, where we make sure we communicate as much as we possibly can, maximum disclosure as I call it, to those families so at least we bring them some form of closure.*
>
> *Currently, the Enquiry Team is producing a Family Liaison Information*

Booklet which will be sent out to all people who may be affected by this work. This is a very significant development, but in addition to that, in terms of the routine of policing now, since 2002 we do have a system of Family Liaison Officers who support and keep members of kin informed on every single homicide we have to deal with. We also use Family Liaison Officers, for example, in fatal road accidents and missing persons enquiries, where we think it is appropriate.

In addition to those experts we also have ... Minority Liaison Officers in every single district to make sure we keep a proper and professional relationship with victims of hate crime and those Minority Liaison Officers also provide support and advice to investigating officers to assist the victims of hate crime and assist the victims to access the support agencies where they can.
It is quite a complicated setup, but it is a fundamental piece of our business. We also do the same, for example, with domestic violence officers, to make sure we have that role covered as well.

In terms of the routine of crime, our Crime Management Unit now write to all victims of crime giving the name of the investigating officer, the crime reference number and advising them in relation to crime prevention advice and the services of our local Crime Prevention Officer. We also liaise very closely and work with Victims Support who can also give advice regarding how their agency can be of help. There is a lot of work being progressed. Can we do better? I think you can always do better at keeping families informed, certainly in the routine of policing, as well as in the more serious cases. I think that the new piece of business for us is dealing with historic cases, where I think we will be judged quite frankly, on how successful we are at keeping victims of those crimes up to speed on what has been going on.'

In response to a question from a Member at the meeting of the Policing Board held on 2 June 2005, the Chief Constable updated the Board on the current position regarding a legal action being taken by former police officers regarding post-traumatic stress. (NB. At a meeting of the Board's Corporate Policy Committee held on 16 September 2004 the details of the defence which would be laid before the court on 17 September 2004 was noted, and at the meeting on 21 April 2005 it was further noted that the Authority/Board had now been removed from the legal action.)

The Minutes of the Policing Board meeting held on 2 June 2005 recorded as follows:

> *The NIAC's 'Ways of Dealing with NI's Past: Interim Report – Victims and Survivors' had been considered by the Board's Working Group which is considering the role of the Board within the policing architecture.*
>
> *The Working Group did not develop a response to the Interim Report. [Rather] discussion at the Working Group focussed on a submission by the Chairman/Vice-Chairman to a [colloquium staged by the School of Religions and Theology and the Irish School of Ecumenics, Trinity College, Dublin, on 10 June 2005,' the theme of which was 'Telling the Truth in Northern Ireland']*

On 16 June 2005 at the Board's Corporate Policy Committee the Chairman gave a brief report on the latter.

At the same Corporate Policy Committee it was noted in respect of the NIAC's Interim Report that:

> 'The Board Group, which was considering the future role of the Board, had considered the NIAC report on ways of dealing with Northern Ireland's past and had agreed that no further action should be taken by the Board at present.'

Prior to the Trinity College Dublin colloquium, the Chief Constable, the Chairman and Vice-Chairman agreed to the contents of a paper very much based on that of 17 June 2003 and of the same title, *'Seeking to Hold the Past in Healthy Balance with the Future'*. The substantive changes to the first paper included:

- The note that the revised paper formed the basis of a submission to the NIAC's inquiry into *'Ways of Dealing with NI's Past'* and that the Committee had published its Interim Report;
- The paragraphs on *the policing context* and *the way forward* as noted by the Board on 1 December 2004 – see above but slightly amended, were incorporated as parts 3 and 4 respectively.

The paper is printed in full as Annex A.

Among *Political Members* on the Policing Board the paper as read to the colloquium was not without its critics, for example Ian Paisley Jnr argued:

'The authors should recognise that the Policing Board is ***not*** *the centre of gravity for any of these matters!... The paper expresses what are essentially*

political views about the past, its conflict past and how to deal with its victims.

The paper appears ... to be making the case for an amnesty for all crime on the pretext the Belfast Agreement released 'prisoners of war' therefore any future process will be an amnesty for those on the wrong side as well as on the paramilitary side. I have never read such drivel before ...'

The views expressed by Ian Paisley Jnr perhaps explain why, at the meeting of the Policing Board held on 30 June 2005, the Board noted that:

> *'The Chairman reminded Members that the Board's Working Group had agreed not to develop a response to the Northern Ireland Affairs Committee Interim Report. The consensus view was that issues concerning dealing with the past would be taken forward by government and the political parties, rather than the Board.'*

Also at the Trinity College Dublin colloquium on 10 June 2005 Chief Constable Hugh Orde read a separate paper *'War is Easy to Declare, Peace is an Elusive Prize'*, in which he argued as follows:

> *[I realize] that in order to deliver 21st century policing in Northern Ireland, we require a radical solution to the past ... [We] need to address [it] more fundamentally and comprehensively ... We need to meet the basic challenge of whether we should in fact remember at all or instead put the past, its pain, conflict and potential for controversy to one side and, as it were, just forget ... I have some compelling reasons - not least from a policing perspective – for insisting that we deal with the past in order to facilitate movement forward ... We need a comprehensive strategy.*
>
> *[Without the latter] demands for public inquiries become the order of the day, with a focus on State collusion and conspiracy. This one-dimensional approach fails to acknowledge the sheer scale of the miserable history, and allows a hierarchy of death to be created where some victims are deemed more important than others. In statistical terms, it is a matter of fact that the majority of re-investigations and enquiries currently underway are focussed on victims of alleged State involvement in the murder in a context where the majority of deaths and injuries resulted from the actions of paramilitary organisations. The impact on other victims is substantial. They feel disenfranchised, and do not see the State pursuing their loved ones' killers with matching vigour ...*

In respect of the concluding paragraphs of the 'Way Forward' of the

Chairman's, Vice-Chairman's and Chief Constable's paper on *'Seeking to Hold the Past in a Healthy Balance with the Future'* as submitted to the NIAC in June 2005 (at Annex A), the Chairman on 15 May 2006 wrote to the NIO Minister of State, Paul Goggins, as follows:

> *'At the March 2006 meeting of the Police Advisory Board (PAB), the issue of 'new initiatives to deal with the past' was discussed. I informed those present of a paper which the then Vice-Chairman of the Board, the Chief Constable and myself had developed and agreed as a way of progressing the debate on dealing with the past. At the end of our discussion at PAB the Minister encouraged those present to get involved in identifying a vehicle for addressing the past and emphasised the importance of finding a resolution to these issues. I wholeheartedly endorse those sentiments and have therefore taken the liberty of circulating the paper which sets out a proposed way forward that Denis Bradley (the then Vice-Chairman), the Chief Constable and I consider helps us find resolution.*
>
> *I acknowledge and appreciate the many differing views of how to tackle the past within the Northern Ireland context and I would like to emphasise that the Commission proposed in the paper is simply a think tank which could, through dialogue with those affected by the past, develop a mechanism for dealing with the past. I would consider that the range of people who should be involved in such dialogue would include families of those killed or injured, including within the police family; representative groups for Victims of Troubles; PSNI; Government and statutory agencies; non-government and community groups. This list is not exhaustive. I would ask you to note that the Commission we have proposed, unlike commissions in other countries, is not the end game or the solution, rather it is the means of finding a satisfactory solution.'*

In a thoughtful and challenging speech, *'Policing the Past to Police the Future'* delivered at Queen's University on 13 November 2006 the Chief Constable commented:

> *'.... It must always be remembered that terrorists killed the vast majority of victims during the Troubles. That is a simple fact (see 'Lives Lost'); it does not mean the State should be excluded from the debate. ... I am charged with moving policing on in a way that increases confidence in all communities. I am determined to provide the*

services necessary to protect them. To do this I need my people to be judged on what they do now, not five years ago, not ten years ago and certainly not over a third of a century ago.

… Father Brian Lennon points out that enquiries into the past may lead to an ***unequal*** *outcome, as they are more likely to focus on abuses by security forces than on those committed by paramilitaries. This current group [The Cory Group of four in Northern Ireland and one in the Republic of Ireland] fall firmly into that category. Indeed if one examines the necessarily broad definition of collusion adopted, this outcome was utterly predictable.*

… As to the costs of public inquiries … in determining how we define the future of Northern Ireland through dealing with the past, it is legitimate, (although difficult and controversial) to challenge how the money is being spent and how much should be spent … I estimate I will be spending at least £2m a year in staff and legal costs to service the current level of demand – probably a lot more from the inquiries that are up and running.

… Current policing will suffer. I find myself between a rock and a hard place. Do I shift resources to look backwards and in so doing put current police operations, and indeed lives at risk? I have to say that I am not prepared to do the latter and consequently run the risk of increasing the time I take to respond to legitimate requests from inquiries.

Some of the implications of the Act (Inquiries Act 2005) are, I think more far-reaching in a strategic police intelligence sense than anyone envisaged. Let me explain. When this legislation is deployed, the Chairman of the inquiry may require a person to produce any documents in his custody that relate to a matter in question at the inquiry … It has to be stated that the notion that people will provide information to police knowing that there is substantial potential for their details to be passed to third parties at some time in the future is simply not going to happen.… So, whilst public inquiries may be a small part of the solution there has to be a better way … I fully accept that [the Cory inquiries] are now inevitable, and I will ensure that all information they need that I own will be made available so they can carry out their task. My basic point is that the piecemeal approach to history is doomed to fail, and be divisive. Why are all other victims denied the opportunity for an equivalent investment in their case? Why should cases that suit some political imperative be advanced over other equally deserving cases. I have been privileged to meet many families from across the divide during my time here, and it is hard to explain why there appears, no, why currently there is a hierarchy of death when it comes to looking backwards. It is worth noting that I confidently predict that the cost of the HET, which is an honourable attempt to examine thousands of cases, will cost substantially less than the legal costs of the latest public enquiries. Indeed whether we can deliver within our timeframe and within resources is something I am looking at. But we will continue to try our best in the hope that in the near future we will see some leadership grip this issue once and for all. If Government are holding back, it may be that a new assembly could grasp this and move it on.'

At the meeting of the Policing Board of 22 March 2007 the Chairman raised the issue of *Dealing With The Past* and called on Mr Trevor Ringland, *Independent Member*, to outline his views on how the issue should be taken forward. Following discussion Members agreed that *'leadership for "dealing with the past" was a matter for consideration by the Northern Ireland Assembly with the Board having an appropriate contribution to make'*.

2.3 The Consultative Group On The Past

In the *public session* of the Policing Board meeting held on 5 July 2007 the Board noted that Secretary of State for Northern Ireland, Peter Hain, had announced on 22 June 2007 the formation of the Independent Consultative Group on the Past. The Group was asked:

- to consult across the community on how Northern Ireland society can best approach the legacy of the events of the past 40 years;
- to make recommendations, as appropriate, on any steps that might be taken to support Northern Ireland society in building a shared future that is not overshadowed by the events of the past; and
- to present a report, which will be published, setting out conclusions to the Secretary of State for Northern Ireland.

The Right Reverend Lord Eames, former Archbishop of Armagh, and Mr Denis Bradley, the first Vice-Chairman of the Policing Board were appointed co-chairs of the Consultative Group on the Past.

On 6 September 2007 the co-chairs of the Consultative Group on the Past issued an open letter encouraging all those affected by the legacy of the events in Northern Ireland over the past 40 years to share their views with the Group. The Policing Board's Corporate Policy, Planning and Performance Committee at its meeting on 20 September 2007 considered the Group's press release of 6 September 2007. The Committee considered the issue of the Board making a corporate response to the Group and following discussion it was agreed that a discussion paper should be drafted to further consider the submission of a corporate response to the Group; it was also suggested that Members might meet informally to discuss the development of a corporate response.

At a dinner hosted by the NIO for Board Members on 2 October 2007 it was evident that, given the high degree of disagreement, it was unrealistic to expect consensus on a corporate response to the Group. The latter was noted at the Policing Board meeting on 1 November 2007 where it was resolved:

- that the *Political Members* of the Board should engage with the Group through their respective political parties;
- that *Independent Members*, including the Chairman and Vice-Chairman of the Board, could meet with the Group in an independent capacity to present their own views as individual Members; and
- that *Independent Members* would discuss whether to make arrangements for a separate meeting with the Group and advise the Chairman accordingly.

At the Board meeting on 6 December 2007 it was noted that *Independent Members* had met to discuss whether they could develop a consensus view on a presentation to the Group and they were not yet ready to decide whether they should meet as a group with the Consultative Group. The Chairman and Vice-Chairman indicated that they planned to meet with the Group during December 2007.

At the meeting of the Policing Board held on 7 February 2008 the Chairman gave a verbal update that he and the Vice-Chairman had had with the Consultative Group on 23 January 2008.

On 12 September 2007 at the Annual Conference of the Police Federation for Northern Ireland, their Chairman Terry Spence commented on the work of the Independent Consultative Group on the Past as follows:

> *'There can be no truth commission included in their recommendations. Especially when one of the leading proponents of the truth commission [presumably Gerry Adams] cannot even admit*

that he was in the IRA … The focus must be moved from how we deal with the past to how we deal with the future.'

At the meeting of the Policing Board's Corporate Policy, Planning and Performance Committee held on 15 May 2008 the Chief Executive informed Members that the co-chairs of the Consultative Group on the Past, having completed an extensive public consultation in January 2008, had delivered a keynote address; a copy of the latter was forwarded to all consultees. The covering letter to the address stressed that its purpose *'was to set out what the Group believes are the key issues society needs to address if we are to move towards a shared future that is not overshadowed by the past.'*

Comments made in the address include the following:

- *There are issues from the past that must be dealt with if we are truly to ensure that we do not repeat the mistakes of the past. Dealing with the past will secure our future.*
- *When we were established our remit was to seek a consensus on the way forward. There is a consensus that we must do things differently.*
- *Many of the arguments and disagreements, especially the definition of a victim or hierarchy of victims, are hurting the very people we should all be striving to help.*
- *In all our consultations it is unclear if Republicans truly appreciate the depth of hurt that exists in the Unionist community … Indeed if the aim of the Republican struggle was to unite Catholic, Protestant and Dissenter, the brutal logic is their violence undermined this aim. … Republicans need to convince their neighbours that they will not take up arms again to advance their political cause …*
- *Republicans and Nationalists believe that Unionists have not come to terms with the reasons for [their broad disillusionment and alienation] from the State and subsequent actions.*
- *Loyalists sought to defend the Union but they killed those they wished to convince had a future within the Union. They [too] need to make it clear to their neighbours that they will not begin their violence again.*
- *The elements of the State, on some occasions, acted outside the law and through handling of intelligence it could even be said innocent people were allowed to die. We cannot ignore that the State sometimes acted illegally. If we are to move out of the past in a healthy way then the State itself needs to acknowledge its full and complex role in the last 40 years … [However, full disclosure has its repercussions].*

- *It is difficult for us not to listen to those experts who are telling us that the reality is that as each day passes securing justice becomes less and less likely.*
- *However, there are other ways of seeking truth that do not include long drawn out judicial processes. What we need is our solution to our problems. Truth and justice are not mutually exclusive but neither are they always attainable.*
- *...If we are to have a future not overshadowed by the past we will require political leadership from the Assembly.*
- *As a Group we are committed to addressing the legacy of the past in a way that will promote a greater goal of reconciliation within and between our people.*

At the Policing Board of 5 February 2009 the Chairman highlighted under 'publications received', inter alia, the *Report of the Consultative Group on the Past*, dated 23 January 2009. The following is the Group's summary of its report's main recommendations.

'***Legacy of the Past and Reconciliation***

- *An independent Legacy Commission should be established to deal with the legacy of the past by combining processes of reconciliation, justice and information recovery. It would have the overarching objective of promoting peace and stability in Northern Ireland.*
- *A Reconciliation Forum should be established through which the Legacy Commission and the Commission for Victims and Survivors for Northern Ireland (CVSNI) would liaise to tackle certain society issues relating to the conflict.*
- *The Legacy Commission should be given a bursary of £100m to tackle these society issues.*

Victims and Survivors

- *The suffering of families from Northern Ireland and Great Britain should be recognised. The nearest relative of someone who died as a result of the conflict in and about Northern Ireland, from January 1966, should receive a one-off ex-gratia recognition payment of £12,000.*
- *The CVSNI should take account of, and address in their work programme, the present and future needs and concerns of victims and survivors, devoting attention to provision of services, funding, healthcare needs and compensation.*
- *The Reconciliation Forum would also have a mandate to promote*

the improvement of services for healthcare issues attributable to the conflict, such as trauma, suicide and addiction.

The Legacy Commission

- *The Chair of the Legacy Commission should be an International Commissioner, who would also have specific responsibility within the Commission for addressing society issues through the Reconciliation Forum, tackling sectarianism, promoting reconciliation and administering the bursary. There would be two other Commissioners.*
- *The mandate of the Legacy Commission would consist of four strands of work:*
    - *Helping society towards a shared and reconciled future, through a process of engagement with community issues arising from the conflict;*
    - *Reviewing and investigating historical cases;*
    - *Conducting a process of information recovery;*
    - *Examining linked or thematic cases emerging from the conflict.*
- *The Legacy Commission's mandate would be for a fixed period of five years.*
- *The Office of the First Minister and deputy First Minister (OFMDFM) should join the British and Irish Governments in implementing this initiative.*

Society Issues

- *Society issues arising from the conflict which should be tackled include: addressing sectarianism; promoting remembering activities; working with young people; providing improved services for healthcare needs; ensuring an even spread of economic benefits; and helping those exiled from Northern Ireland during the conflict to return.*
- *The Reconciliation Forum should help to address these issues by analysing activity undertaken; considering the need for further activity; giving advice to Government and others; advising on strategies and on the development and delivery of services; and deciding on priority areas of activity.*
- *The Legacy Commission should act as a champion for these society issues.*
- *The Legacy Commission should take the lead in ensuring that*

sectarianism continues to be addressed, including through setting the direction for the debate and by highlighting the contribution that all sectors of society can make.

- *The Legacy Commission should engage specifically with the Christian churches in Northern Ireland to encourage them to review and rethink their contribution to a non-sectarian future in the light of their past, particularly in the area of education.*
- *The guidance produced by the Quigley-Hamilton working group, to eliminate discrimination against those with conflict-related convictions, should be incorporated into statute and made applicable to the provision of goods, facilities and services as well as recruitment.*

Processes of Justice and Information Recovery

- *A new independent Unit dealing with historical cases would be created within the Legacy Commission, which would continue to review and investigate historical cases, backed by police powers. This would constitute the second strand of the Commission's work.*
- *The new Review and Investigation Unit would take over the work of the Historical Enquiries Team and the Police Ombudsman's Unit dealing with the historical cases. The need for these would fall away when the new Unit is established. The New Unit would build on the work they have done to date.*
- *The process of recovering information of importance to relatives (information recovery) would be separated from the investigation procedure and be subject to a distinct process within the Legacy Commission under a separate Commissioner. This would constitute the third strand of the Commission's work.*
- *In the fourth strand of its work, the Legacy Commission would examine themes arising from the conflict which remain of public concern, such as specific areas of paramilitary activity, or alleged collusion. This thematic examination would take place without public hearings. This would facilitate more open and frank disclosure and avoid the constant publicity of present inquiry proceedings.*

- *There would be no new public inquiries. The question whether to proceed with the promised Finucane Inquiry is a matter for the British Government but the issues raised by this case could be dealt with by the Legacy Commission.*
- *The outstanding inquests would remain with the Coroner's Service. Criminal case reviews would continue to be pursued through the Criminal Cases Review Commission.*
- *The Group is not proposing an amnesty but recommends that the Legacy Commission itself make recommendations on how a line might be drawn at the end of its five year mandate so that Northern Ireland might best move to a shared future.*

Remembering

- *The Legacy Commission should, through the Reconciliation Forum, support CVSNI in facilitating and encouraging the telling of stories, including by young people, about the impact of the conflict on individuals and communities; and the stories of intra-communal difference.*
- *CVSNI should also be supported in developing the existing ways in which the conflict and its impact are remembered. This should include the development of educational projects; providing support and guidance for those facilitating remembering projects in line with certain criteria; and promoting the value of remembering across society as a means of achieving reconciliation.*
- *Future storytelling initiatives should be developed taking account of certain criteria.*
- *Full support should be given by government, the private and voluntary sector, including the churches, to the continuation of the annual Day of Reflection, initiated by Healing Through Remembering, on 21 June each year. Consideration should be given to renaming the event a Day of Reflection and Reconciliation.*
- *Each year, on or around the Day of Reflection and Reconciliation, the First Minister and deputy First Minister should together make a keynote address to the Northern Ireland Assembly and invited guests, reflecting on the past in a positive way and confirming their commitment to lead Northern Ireland society towards a shared and reconciled future.*

- *The Reconciliation Forum should take the lead in implementing an initiative, at the end of the five year mandate of the Legacy Commission, whereby Northern Ireland, with the support of the two Governments and the Northern Ireland Assembly, should conduct a ceremony remembering the past and all those who suffered during the conflict.*
- *The Group therefore recommends that the Commission should, at the end of its work, challenge the people of Northern Ireland, including political parties and whatever remnant or manifestation of paramilitary groups remain, to sign a declaration to the effect that they will never again kill or injure others on political grounds.*
- *A shared memorial to remember the conflict in and about Northern Ireland should be kept under consideration by the Reconciliation Forum and criteria should be observed, in working towards a shared memorial conducive to reconciliation. The Legacy Commission should, at the end of its five year life span, make recommendations to Government in this regard.'*

In the *public session* of the Policing Board's meeting on 5 February 2009 *Political Member* Ian Paisley Jnr commented as follows:

> *'Thank you Chairman. With regards to the Eames/Bradley issue, it appears to me that from the thrust of what has been said generally, there is almost a working assumption that the Eames/Bradley recommendations are going to be implemented. I think that is actually the wrong working assumption. I do not detect either the political will to implement Eames/Bradley and I do not detect the financial ability to implement Eames/Bradley and I think therefore that working assumption should may be set to the side. Maybe I am wrong in picking that up but it is just something that I assume.'*

No, Ian Paisley Jnr was not wrong; he got it absolutely right. Eames/Bradley appears to have been buried with the tacit consent of the main parties. Both the importance of the issue and the thoughtfulness with which it was addressed by the Eames/Bradley Team should have ensured that it received a constructive debate.

2.4 On-The-Runs

With respect to the 'On-the-Runs' Dan Keenan in the *Irish Times* of 14 October

2005 reported that the British Government was expected shortly to publish legislation dealing with paramilitary fugitives:

> *'… The measures will "deal with the position of individuals connected with paramilitary crimes committed before the Belfast Agreement", Northern Secretary Peter Hain said yesterday.*
> *In a statement to the House of Commons he said the British government would not introduce an amnesty. However he forecast that the proposals "will be painful for many people" in the unionist community.*
>
> *He stressed: "I fully understand this. But the government believes that it is a necessary part of the process of closing the door on violence forever."'*

On 9 November 2005 the United Kingdom Government introduced in Parliament the Northern Ireland (Offences) Bill: *'This legislation will bring forward the Government's proposals to deal with the outstanding question of terrorist suspects on-the-run (OTRs).'* The Notes to Editors in the accompanying press release summarised the legislation:

> *'The legislation sets out the two-stage process whereby individuals may apply for a certificate of eligibility and be brought before a special tribunal.*
>
> *The scheme covers offences committed in relation to terrorism and the affairs of Northern Ireland before the Belfast Agreement. This includes offences committed in any part of the UK.*
> *The scheme will be open to those who are on the run for relevant offences and to those charged or convicted of such offences during the period of the scheme.*
>
> *The criteria for eligibility for the scheme are that:*
> - *the person does not support a specified organisation;*
> - *the person is not concerned or likely to be concerned in the commission, preparation or instigation of acts of terrorism;*
> - *the person has not been convicted of a terrorist-related offence committed on or after 10 April 1998; and*
> - *no sentence of imprisonment for a term of five years or more has been imposed on the person on conviction of an offence committed on or after 10 April 1998.*
>
> *Applications will be made to a certification commissioner and eligibility will be determined according to strict criteria. Certificates can be*

cancelled by the Secretary of State if their terms are broken. Challenges to decisions of the certification commissioner and the Secretary of State will take place before specially appointed Appeals Commissioners.

The certification commissioner will have an explicit obligation to provide a liaison to victims and provide information, where possible, about relevant cases.

The certificate will identify the offences to which the certificate applies. It does not apply generally, but only to the offences listed on the certificate.

The certificate will grant the person exemptions from certain police powers, including arrest, questioning and remand, in relation to listed offences. The exemptions will have little effect for anyone who qualifies because they have been charged with an offence; the investigation for that offence will be complete, and investigations into other offences will be allowed to continue.

Any prosecution for a listed offence will take place in a Special Tribunal set up under this legislation. Prosecutions will be brought by a Special Prosecutor and the normal prosecution tests will apply. The Special Tribunal will have all the powers and procedures of the Crown Court sitting without a jury. The defendant will not have to attend the trial, but otherwise the trial will follow the same pattern as a normal trial on indictment.

The Special Prosecutor will have an explicit obligation to provide a liaison to victims during the course of any trial.

Conviction and sentence before the Special Tribunal may be appealed before a Special Appeals Tribunal, also established by this legislation. In the event of a conviction, the person will be eligible to receive a licence. The terms of the licence are similar to those under the Northern Ireland (Sentences) Act 1998 (the Early Release Scheme). A person given a life sentence will not be granted a licence if he is deemed to be a danger to the public. No licence can be granted until the person complies with requirements in relation to providing fingerprints and non-intimate samples.

The licences will be subject to suspension and revocation if the conditions are broken, in the same way as Early Release Scheme licences.

Conditions for holding a licence are that:

- *the person does not support a specified organisation;*
- *he is not concerned or likely to be concerned in the commission, preparation or instigation of acts of terrorism;*
- *he has not been convicted of a terrorist-related offence committed on or after 10 April 1998;*
- *no sentence of imprisonment for a term of five years or more has been imposed on him on conviction of an offence committed on or after 10 April 1998; and*
- *the person has not at any time been a supporter of an organisation which was not a specified organisation at the time of the grant of a licence but has become a specified organisation.'*

When announcing the legislation the NIO Minister David Hanson stated:

> *'The Government is very aware that this is a difficult issue, and one which will be hard for many people to accept. However, sometimes it is necessary to make difficult decisions in the interests of entrenching the benefits of peace. This is one such occasion.'*

The Policing Board at its meeting on 7 December 2005 agreed that the Board's *'Working Group on Community Restorative Justice should consider the Northern Ireland (Offences) Bill (the proposed on-the-run legislation) and make recommendations to the Board concerning a corporate response'.*

2.5 The Interim Commissioner For Victims And Survivors

On 24 October 2005 Secretary of State Peter Hain announced the appointment of Mrs Bertha McDougall as the Interim Commissioner for Victims and Survivors of the Troubles. In his 'Notes to Editors' he stated that the Interim Commissioner would carry out the following duties:

- *'Review arrangements for service delivery and coordination of services for victims and survivors across departments and agencies, identifying any gaps in service provision.*
- *Review how well the current funding arrangements in relation to services and grants paid to victims and survivors groups and individual victims and survivors are addressing need. At present around 50 groups are in receipt of government grants.*
- *Consider the modalities of establishing a Victims and Survivors Forum.'*

He added that he expected the Interim Commissioner to produce a report within the year ... and that the legislation to establish a Commissioner on a longer term basis would be introduced. The Secretary of State followed up this announcement three days later when he announced extra funding of £1.5m to support victims and survivors of the Troubles through the Northern Ireland Memorial Fund. And on 21 July 2006 the Government announced the launching of a public consultation on its proposals to enact legislation to establish a Commissioner for Victims and Survivors.

2.6 The Enniskillen Bombing

At the meeting of the Policing Board held on 2 June 2005 Mr Sam Foster, *Political Member* (UUP), asked the Chief Constable the following question:

> *'Thank you Chairman. Chief Constable, can you give me a report on the situation towards bringing before court, those who murdered 12 citizens in the Cenotaph bomb in Enniskillen on 8 November 1987 - that is almost 18 years ago?'*

The Chief Constable delegated the answer to ACC Crime Operations, Sam Kinkaid:

> *"Chairman, it is recognised that the incidents that led to the murder of the 12 people attending the Cenotaph on the 8 November 1987 was one of the most abhorrent in the history of Northern Ireland and police investigations therefore, have continued to pursue every avenue right up to and including the present day. In 2004 I led the investigation, subject to a further review, to see whether there were any new evidential lines of enquiry and the review officers made a number of recommendations that are now being actively pursued.*
>
> *Detectives from Crime Operations Department have recently sought to trace and re-interview some 111 people as part of that process and put their recollections into context. Some 80 witnesses have been seen to date and efforts will continue to be made to speak to the remainder and some additional 45 witnesses identified by those already spoken to, these are new witnesses that have come to light. This will be, of course, a painstaking process in which every piece of information will have to be thoroughly analysed. In addition to tracing scores of new witnesses, other investigators were concluding some of the details in liaison with colleagues in An Garda Siochana. This is presently being pursued and we remain committed to ensuring that where there is sufficient evidence to bring charges that those persons responsible for this particular crime are brought to justice".*

At the 40th meeting in public of the Policing Board held on 1 March 2006

Political Member, Mr Sam Foster, put the following question on the Enniskillen bombing to the Chief Constable:

> *'Thank you Chairman, Continuous disappointment. Carnage at Enniskillen Cenotaph, Remembrance Sunday almost 19 years ago, 12 dead many injured. Can the Chief Constable update the situation or are the Enniskillen victims suffering from non-remembrance?*
>
> ***Chief Constable, Sir Hugh Orde**:*
> *"I will ask Chief Superintendent, Crime Operations to deal with that but as I mentioned in my opening remarks, the people around this table have taken historic enquiries extremely seriously which is why we now have a fully funded and fully staffed group of people capable of dealing with these offences but I will ask Chief Superintendent, Crime Operations to deal with the detail."*
>
> ***Chief Superintendent, Crime Operations**:*
> *"Crime Operations Branch, our C2 people continue to actively pursue and deal with lines of enquiry in relation to the Enniskillen bombing. Just recently, we have identified some new witnesses and they have been interviewed. When those lines of enquiry are finished the case will then be handed to the Historical Enquiries Team, this has already been raised. As you know, that has been designed to provide a thorough and independent reappraisal of unsolved cases. They have a family centred approach, obviously to seek to address as far as possible the questions of families and issues that remain outstanding. Their governing principle will be maximum disclosure obviously subject to legal guidelines. Now as a general rule, cases will be examined on chronological order basis, the only exceptions to that will be where there are cases which are already opened. I can assure you that the Enniskillen case is one that will be treated as a case that is already opened ..."*

2.7 A Private Day Of Reflection

At the meeting of the Policing Board held on 6 June 2007 the Board considered a paper (from which the following paragraphs are drawn) concerning an initiative proposed by Healing Through Remembering (HTR) for a 'private' Day of Reflection. The latter is a cross community and cross political project made up of individuals from differing backgrounds which was established in 2001 to consider ways in which issues arising from the 'conflict in and about Northern Ireland' could be addressed. The project has made six recommendations which form a series of linked strategies to promote healing through remembering including the establishment of:

- a network of commemoration and remembering projects;
- a collective storytelling and archiving process;
- a permanent memorial museum;
- a HTR initiative to take forward the implementation; and
- a day of reflection.

HTR established a Day of Reflection sub-group and in September 2006 they prepared a discussion paper, *'A Day of Private Reflection: Discussion Paper and Proposal'*. HTR announced the event on 4 October 2006 in Armagh and invited feedback. After their consultation with various bodies including victims and survivors, church groups, faith groups, trade unions and employers groups, they felt the event would make a contribution to '*enabling society to deal with the legacy of the conflict and to move forward to a better future'*.

The basic concept for the Day, which is a voluntary opportunity, is to provide a 'private' space and time for everyone to think about the consequences of the conflict, and to begin to recognise and acknowledge the suffering caused, and to consider the role of society during the conflict. Suggested activities include a moment of silence, saying a prayer, or visiting a place of worship or other reflective place.

The intention is that the first event be a Day of Private Reflection. This pilot is to give people an opportunity to reflect individually, as a family or a group. HTR intend to provide guidance materials, counselling and other support services. HTR intends to evaluate the occasion with a view to repeating the event in future years in a more public arena.

It was resolved that the Board should support the Healing Through Remembering Day of Private Reflection and that a press release to that effect should be issued on or about 21 June 2007.

2.8 The Saville Report On Bloody Sunday

On 15 June 2010 Lord Saville published his Bloody Sunday Report. On 19 June 2010 *The Economist* commented as follows:

> *"After 12 years, more than 900 witnesses and £195m ($288m), the findings of Lord Saville, a High Court judge charged by the British government with establishing the truth about what happened on January 30 1972 in the Bogside area of Londonderry, have finally been made public. His main conclusion – that British paratroopers had no*

justification for killing any of the 13 men who died, some shot from behind, on what has come to be known as Bloody Sunday – will have a profound effect on relations between the British government and Irish nationalists. That effect will be entirely positive.

Relations have already improved immeasurably in recent years, but the inquiry's conclusions, painful though they are for the authorities and the army, have removed an historic and deeply held nationalist grievance. They amounted to an exorcism of ghosts at large for almost four decades, removing at a stroke a significant Anglo-Irish irritant.

Nationalists and republicans, who had been nervous about [Prime Minister} Cameron's professed leanings towards the unionist cause, said they were impressed by his speed in endorsing Lord Saville's stark conclusions.

Unionist opinion was divided. After the report was made public, leaders of the three main Protestant churches met relatives of the Bloody Sunday victims at a memorial in the Bogside. There, using rhetoric of a type rarely heard in Northern Ireland, they declared: "A cloud that has been hanging over this city for almost four decades has begun to lift ... We dare to believe that this can be a decisive turning-point in reaching out to one another."

Many Protestants, however, complained that the misdeeds of the British army had been broadcast to the world while the IRA had virtually escaped criticism. Most of the relatives of IRA victims, they said, are suffering in silence without public recognition or prime ministerial apologies. For those who lost friends and family to these killers, the extensive investigation of controversial incidents involving the army contrasts sourly with the lack of attention paid to their own tragedies.

Of the 3,700 who died in the Troubles, 1,800 were killed by the IRA, and around a thousand by extreme Protestant groups. The army killed 300. About 250,000 regular soldiers served in Northern Ireland over more than 30 years....

On 16 June 2010 in *The Financial Times*, John Lloyd movingly commented on Lord Saville's Bloody Sunday Report:

'The details are now likely to be as clear as they will ever be. While the prime minister's statement that such a sprawling inquiry will

never be launched again testifies to the general view that it has been excessive, it may still have a value – if, that is, the response to it builds not on the spectres of the past but on the promise that the past decade of (mostly) peace has – often shakily – contained.

The details reveal a mind-set on all sides of bitterness, bigotry and a belief that the other could be defeated, as bloodily as necessary. There is no question that the IRA initiated most of the bloodshed during the Troubles; that the Unionist community had allowed discrimination to flourish for the half-century of Northern Ireland's existence; that the British government had, until the Troubles flared in 1968, simply ignored the issue. There is no question, finally, that trained killers in British uniform ran amok.

There will inevitably be calls by nationalists for prosecutions of the Paras, which in turn would lead to tit-for-tat calls for prosecutions of suspected IRA killers. Yet there is too much at stake to take refuge in past grievances. A new government whose leader has faced up to the doleful duty of blaming his country's soldiers for perpetrating a horror (on a day when two more of them died in Afghanistan) could use the findings to draw a line – by an act of general contrition.

Contrition is central to Christianity, and thus may commend itself to communities whose faith is stronger than anywhere else in these islands. As an expression of intense remorse, with at least a tacit recognition of guilt, it is a recourse for the government, for the military, for communities and for former terrorists.

Such an act should be public, ceremonial, even dramatic. It would involve leaders of all parties; would recognise the tragedies that have beset the relationship between Britain and Ireland; would underpin a new equality of two old nations. It should proceed from a deeper understanding of past failures than many have allowed themselves to date. If done with courage and imagination, it might yet be worth £200m.

Since the first IRA ceasefire in 1994 there have been any number of discussions, conferences and documents seeking to draw up a balance-sheet of the Troubles. None has come close to commanding widespread support, and some have produced much anger. One suggestion, to give £12,000 to the relatives of everyone – terrorist or not – who was killed, caused a furious uproar.

An enormous investigation along Bloody Sunday lines will not be mounted again because the time it took and the costs it ran up were prohibitive. Some lower profile inquiries are under way now, but with rules that impose strict limits on the scope of the proceedings.

The Saville inquiry, meanwhile, has left significant loose ends. A notable one is whether prosecutions should be brought against those soldiers whom the judge came close to accusing of unlawful killing and perjury.

The idea of plunging into new legal thickets is daunting, especially since it might well prove hard to convert Lord Saville's findings into convictions against individuals. And few want to pursue soldiers, even if they were guilty of serious wrongdoing, when virtually all IRA members convicted of terrorist offences were long ago set free as part of the peace process. Unionists are opposed to prosecutions. Most nationalists are too, considering that, with the pronouncements of the judge and the prime minister, truth has been told and honour satisfied.'

Speaking on Wednesday, 13 October 2010, Lord Carswell, former Chief Justice of Northern Ireland, told the House of Lords during a debate on the findings of the Bloody Sunday Report that there would be no further inquiries into killings during the Troubles because Northern Ireland *'badly needs stability.'*

"People have been hurt – many badly and some dreadfully. Much can and should be done to help them in various ways.

However, as a society we badly need stability. One of the best ways of achieving that would be a long period with as little disturbance as possible. Furthermore, Northern Ireland is now in the process of tackling the many problems of today. It needs all the impulse and creativity that it can summon, untrammelled by the weight of old divisions and antipathies.

To this end, the talents and energies, both emotional and practical, of its people must be harnessed. That can only be for the public good.

Like all societies riven by divisions and strife, Northern Ireland has to put them behind it if it is to flourish. In that, increasing prosperity can only be a useful lubricant. If people in countries with problems such as those experienced by Croatia can do it with some success … we can do it.

If we are to develop as a mature and peaceful society, it is better that we should do so without inquiries, which are commonly so prolonged and often controversial, and may produce too little real enlightenment in the end.

To reiterate the cliché: it is time to move on.'

On 17 April 2013 *The Belfast Telegraph* confirmed that the United Kingdom Government was considering releasing previously classified documents from the Troubles era as part of its contribution to *Dealing With The Past*. The paper clarified the background:

'Last December the Government published Sir Desmond de Silva's report into the 1989 murder of Pat Finucane. It broke new ground by publishing a large number of previously classified documents, which resulted in the Prime Minister apologising to the Finucane family for the State's role in the killing. The Finucane family still demand a public enquiry.'

Chapter Three
Reviewing Unsolved Murders

On the back of the Police Ombudsman's recommendations as contained in her *'Report on the Investigation of Matters Relating to the Omagh Bombing of 15 August 1998'* the Board agreed that HMIC David Blakey oversee *'The Review of Terrorist Linked Murder Inquiries'*. The eventual title of the report was his *'Report on Murder Investigation for the Chief Constable of the Police Service of Northern Ireland'*, completed in 2003. HMIC Blakey commented on 're-investigations' as follows:

> '5.4 *the European Court of Human Rights has interpreted Article 2 of HRA (Right to life) as placing a responsibility on the State, including the police to provide a thorough and effective investigation capable of leading to the identification and punishment of those responsible for murders.*
>
> 5.5 *Since the beginning of the Troubles (1969) Northern Ireland has suffered an unprecedented level of violence and murder. The volume and frequency of deaths has created a legacy for policing today. A consequence of this has been an increasing demand by relatives of victims for information concerning the present state of police investigations.*
>
> > *"Many of these cases are protracted in nature, but an encouraging (yet disconcerting) trend is starting to emerge where there is pressure from the relatives of murder victims from the Troubles, to reopen and further investigate "old, unsolved" cases, some going back to the 1970s". (Annual HMIC inspection of PSNI 2002)*
>
> 5.6 *PSNI has received a number of letters from relatives of victims killed during the Troubles requesting an assessment of the progress of the investigation in accordance with Article 2 Human Rights Act. These letters are being received both at DCUs and at Headquarters and the response varies from department to department. Some cases prompt a re-investigation whilst others become subject to a desk top review. There is a need for corporate policy in reacting to these enquiries.'*

The Board Corporate Policy Committee at its meeting on 20 February 2003 noted that the Chief Constable had publicly raised the issue of the allocation of police investigative resources to re-examine 'historical crimes'. The Committee considered that this was an issue that the Board might wish to discuss with the Chief Constable in more detail. At its meeting on 5 March 2003 the Board agreed that a question should be put to him on this issue. At the *public session* of the Policing Board meeting on 6 October 2004 the following question was asked, and answers given on '*unsolved murders*':

> *Independent Member Mr Barry Gilligan:*
>
> *"Chief Constable, the Board notes from a statement by the Secretary of State to the Labour Party Conference that Government proposes to allocate a sum of money to the PSNI over a three to four year period in order to fund the Serious Crime Review team in reviewing unsolved murders, the number of which we know is very considerable and still a cause of great hurt in this community. Can you clarify for us how you propose to go about this work and how you propose to staff the team to do it?"*
>
> *Chief Constable, Hugh Orde:*
>
> *"I have a number of points to make on this. First, it is our initiative. It was driven by the chief officer team and has been for the last two years in negotiation with the Northern Ireland Office and the Secretary of State because we saw it as being extremely important. It is back to you cannot move on until we deal with history sort of debate. We are very pleased to see as a result of our efforts the Northern Ireland Office is looking to supply us with additional funding to deal with this business so we do not have to draw from the current police budget which is clearly necessary to deal with current policing issues.*
>
> *This is not any sort of replacement for the wider debate around truth and reconciliation issues and all those sorts of things which are being led by the Secretary of State and are out-with our responsibility. This is simply to get sufficient funding to put another unit in place, in addition to our Serious Crime Review team, to assess all the unsolved crimes, including all our unsolved murders of police officers, to see where we have evidential opportunities that we can then pursue. Currently I have not been made aware of the sum of money available. I am told it will be sufficient for the task. The way of structuring it will*

be to second a small number of officers from other police services, if I can find them. I think there will need to be an independent element to this and to staff this with retired high quality detectives to review all the cases we have, to look at the forensic exhibits available and to take advantage of the advances in science specifically, that may well give us evidence we can now pursue through a legal process, which we did not have available to us at the time.

Sam Kinkaid will lead on the day to day running of this unit. It is very important and we are very pleased we have got this far, so quickly. I would hope to be able to come to the Board very soon and tell you exactly what the numbers are but Sam may want to explain further, if that is useful."

At the meeting of the Policing Board held on 7 April 2005 the second press release drawn to Members' attention had been issued by the Northern Ireland Office (NIO) on behalf of Secretary of State Paul Murphy regarding the creation of a new unit within the PSNI to review unsolved deaths. The Secretary of State stated:

"The Government is committed to doing all that it can to help Northern Ireland deal with its troubled past and our pledge to provide the resources to look at unresolved deaths underpins that commitment. We believe that Northern Ireland needs a tailored approach to deal with the pain, grief and anger associated with its past. Part of this approach is the need to address, in a systematic and comprehensive way, all of the unresolved deaths that took place during the Troubles.

The work of the Serious Crime Review Team (SCRT) within the PSNI is an important part of this. It has undertaken ground-breaking work in assessing the prospects for cases to be reinvestigated with the possibility of a judicial outcome, and where it is not possible, in considering ways in which as much information as possible can be made available to the relatives of victims.

Today's announcement will allow the Chief Constable to establish a new unit and expand this work to cover all unresolved deaths [estimated to be 1,800 from 1969 up to the signing of the Agreement in 1998] in a way that will command the confidence of the wider community. It also supports the establishment of a dedicated team in Forensic Science Northern Ireland to provide comprehensive forensic advice to the review.

This is sensitive, painstaking and complex work and in many cases is unlikely to lead to any prosecutions. But it is important work if we are to provide answers to the questions so many people have about the death of their loved ones.'

The press release contained the following 'Note to Editors':

- *The new ring-fenced Review Unit created by the Chief Constable will be headed by a recently retired Commander from the Metropolitan Police, Dave Cox. In addition the head of investigation is a seconded Detective Superintendent, Phil James, who previously worked in the Stevens' team. Detective Superintendent James has full policing powers on secondment to the PSNI working for the Chief Constable, and will be subject to the Code of Ethics and the Ombudsman's regime;*
- *The Unit will be staffed by a mix of serving and retired officers from PSNI and GB forces on an agency basis;*
- *A key part of the process will involve the disclosure of appropriate information to families of victims;*
- *PSNI will create a dedicated intelligence team working to the Review Unit;*
- *There will be some mechanism to ensure an effective review process and public confidence;*
- *All complaints about actions by PSNI (including seconded) officers attached to the Unit will be subject to investigation by the Police Ombudsman in the normal way. This would not extend to agency staff as they will not be exercising police powers.*
- *The Review Unit, which will be part of Crime Operations (C8), will be responsible for carrying out the Minimum Standards Assessment (MSA), Preliminary Case Assessment (PSA) and Deferred Reviews. C8 will also have dedicated Murder Investigation Teams where cases are thought appropriate for reinvestigation.'*

At the *public session* of the Policing Board held on 7 April 2005 *Independent Member* Mrs Pauline McCabe asked the Chief Constable the following question:

> *"Could you explain what criteria are applied to the selection of ex officers to assist with the review of historic cases? Could you also explain what measures you are implementing to optimise confidence in the reviews of cases, where there are particular family or public concerns and also whether you have now established a Gold team or teams with an oversight role and who would be represented on those teams?"*

The Chief Constable replied:

"In terms of selection of both serving and ex-police officers, the approach will be, we need to find people who have the integrity and the skills for the posts we are going to advertise. We have just put out an advert as Stage 1 across the UK and Ireland to see what sort of a response we get.

In particular, in terms of part of C8 which will be the Special Cases Unit, we will have a substantial number of seconded officers and agency staff from outside the PSNI to give that independent element to the investigations where there are particular concerns, but I think it is worth remembering, that in many cases, there will not be particular concerns, people just want their cases reviewed.

I think one of the key areas will be family liaison and we will be attaching a number of our family liaison staff to C8 and a number will come from outside forces. I am also working with developing a specific training programme to develop new thinking around how we handle family liaison across 2,000 plus unsolved killings, which has never been tried before in the history of policing, to my knowledge. The reason we put C8 into Crime Operations group under Sam Kinkaid is to ensure maximum co-operation between its work and other officers who can add value, be it surveillance or intelligence officers or investigation of serious crime. In my view that should routinely remove the need for any more Gold groups unless we need one in a specific case.

The Board is well aware of the amount of oversight I am already subject to. I am not attracted by having an additional Oversight Group per se looking at C8 because each case will be so different, it will require a bespoke response and I am happy to engage at that level, through Sam Kinkaid, when we think it is necessary to put some IAG above it, or a Gold group above it, in particular cases and we have a record of doing that where it needs to take place.

I think it also worth remembering that C8, in terms of going from nothing happening to a lot happening, I am confident that we will get the structure right. It is under the command of Sam Kinkaid, my ACC Crime Operations. It will be headed by two officers, one retired officer and one seconded from the Metropolitan Police, both of whom have substantial experience in dealing with historic cases.

We drove this plan and we drove the whole idea of reinvestigating all these crimes. We got to a point where government have given us the funds, we have been supported by the Policing Board and others in getting to this stage and I think that shows a substantial commitment on our part to do this properly and as well as we possibly can.

That is where we are but if it would be helpful, I am more than happy to do a presentation to the Board and bring the leaders of C8 in to do a presentation on how we think it will work in terms of the finer detail when perhaps we could explore some of the concerns in greater detail."

Chairman, Professor Sir Desmond Rea:
"I think that would be very useful Chief Constable."

Above reference was made to a separate speech *'War is Easy, Peace is an Elusive Prize'* in June 2005 in which the Chief Constable argued in particular that he had:

> *'... some compelling reasons – not least from a policing perspective – for focussing on the present ... My task is to deliver a service that is fit for purpose and structured in a way that it focusses on a community policing style, underpinned by an intelligence led approach to long term problem solving that enables it to perform against targets and, through the National Intelligence Model protect communities from crime ... Action, therefore is needed if policing is not to be dragged backwards ...I and senior colleagues have worked closely with the NIO to seek to formalise and fund a special unit to review old cases – the Historical Enquiries Team (HET).'*

He then went on helpfully to address the questions 'how will the HET work?' and where do the main challenges lie? He accepted that policing and the HET was '*only part of the complex equation that will sum to a comprehensive solution to the past'*.

At the meeting of the Board's Corporate Policy Committee held on 20 October 2005, Mr David Cox, Head of HET, and Detective Superintendent Phil James, made a comprehensive presentation to Members on the purpose of the HET, the extent of its task, its analytical database, the potential areas of opportunity, its prioritisation policy, its critical milestones moving forward, its five phase process (collection/assessment/review/investigation/closure) and other stakeholders.

On 20 January 2006 Secretary of State Peter Hain welcomed the formal launch of the HET: *'Government, through the provision of additional funding to set up the HET, is committed to addressing unanswered questions for as many families as possible'.*

The Board visited the HET on 19 October 2006 and received a presentation covering the scale of their task, to whom they were accountable, and how they prioritised cases. In subsequent discussion Members raised issues around managing the expectations of families and police officers; access to information; the fact that where they implicated someone who was released under the Good Friday Agreement they could not take any action or disclose this to the family concerned and the subsequent need for the truth and reconciliation process to be brought back up the agenda; their need to also engage with retired officers; extremely high public expectations and the need to manage these and provide clarity on the role of the Team.

At the 6 December 2007 *public session* of the Policing Board *Political Member* Alex Maskey (Sinn Fein) posed the following question, '*Why are cases taken out of historical sequence by the HET?'* By agreement he was given the following written response by the Chief Constable:

> *'The HET have in place a prioritisation policy, which is underpinned by the general rule of allocating cases on a chronological basis. Exceptions to the rule are as follows:*

- ***Previously opened investigations** – where some cases were already in the process of review by the PSNI Serious Crime Review Team prior to the establishment of HET; these cases have been adopted by HET and taken out of the chronological process.*
- ***Humanitarian considerations** – in some cases, surviving relatives are themselves very ill or infirm and exceptions to the chronological process are made on the basis of individual circumstances.*
- ***Cases involving issues of Serious Public Interest** – at the direction of the Chief Constable, certain cases are taken out of the chronological process if there is an issue of confidence in policing; an example is the Operation Ballast cases reported on by OPONI.*
- ***Linked series of murders** – when reviewing a case, if links are established to another case it is brought forward for contemporaneous review for practical investigative reasons'.*

At the meeting of the Policing Board held on 6 December 2007 *Political Member* Alex Maskey (Sinn Fein) asked the following question: *'What is the operational relationship between the HET and [the PSNI's] C8?'* Mr Dave Cox,

Head of the HET, replied as follows:

> *"When the [HET] project was under assessment between April 2005 and November 2005, it was given a designation of C8. This was purely an administrative process, as it was initially thought when we were scoping the project, that it might be part of Crime Operations Department which has departments C1 – C7. However, as the scoping of the project developed it became clear from consultation with community groups, from government organisations and families themselves, that the HET needed to demonstrate some operational independence from the PSNI to reassure some sections of the community and also individual families in certain cases.*
>
> *The Chief Constable therefore decided that the Unit would sit outside Crime Operations and other PSNI structures and I, as the Director of the Unit, would be accountable to him for operational decisions. So, therefore, the Historic Enquiries Team is what C8 might have been, but we do not sit within the Crime Operations department.*
>
> *I wonder if perhaps your question was around an operational relationship between us and C2 Department which is the current Murder Investigation Teams. ... Just briefly, we have a number of cases within the PSNI where, before the inception of the Historic Enquiries Team, the Murder Investigation Teams of Crime Operations were relooking at those cases, and in some cases advanced investigations were underway. It is good operational practice that you do not transfer current investigations, and therefore those cases were retained under the auspices of the C2 Department until their completion where, if there is no prosecution coming from them, they will be re-examined again by the HET review process."*

One year in to the scheduled six year life of the HET, the BBC reported on 23 May 2006, that the HET *'team set up to investigate thousands of the Troubles so-called cold cases believe that they have been set an all but impossible task'*; that they would need more money than the £34m allocated and more time. At the Policing Board's Corporate Policy, Planning and Performance Committee held on 15 June 2006, the Chief Constable gave a detailed briefing in relation to the police managerial resource implications for PSNI in providing further requirements of Public Inquiries (i.e. Robert Hamill, Rosemary Nelson, and Billy Wright) and the casework of the HET. The Committee, having discussed the appointment of an additional Assistant

Chief Constable (ACC), resolved under delegated authority that an additional ACC post be created.

At the *public session* of the Policing Board held on 5 October 2006 the Chief Constable, having been questioned by *Political Members* in respect of lost files impinging on the work of the HET, replied:

> *"[Whilst] we have certainly not recovered everything we had hoped to recover through the searches we have undertaken, ... we have found some relevant documentation for nearly every single case and police documentation for over 92% of the 3,268 cases ... Every family we engage with will be told exactly what we have recovered and what we think is missing ..."*

With respect to the funding of 'historical enquiries', the Members of the Policing Board were provided with helpful clarification, from the Northern Ireland Office at official level, in September 2006. (It was as set out in the following five paragraphs.)

On 8 March 2005, the then Secretary of State announced additional funding to the Chief Constable to set up the Historical Enquiries Team whose remit was to complete a review of unresolved deaths in Northern Ireland, due to the security situation, from 1968 to April 1998.

At that time, based on police research, a total of £32m over a six year period was allocated to the unresolved deaths project with the HET receiving the largest portion, £24.2m. The remainder was allocated to the Forensic Science Agency in Northern Ireland (FSNI) for their necessary forensic input. It was then identified that there was a need for consequential additional funding for the Public Prosecution Service (PPS), bringing the total funding to £34m over six years.

When originally considering the Chief Constable's case for this initiative, the Government had been of the view this work would be carried out by the police. However, following discussions concerning the role that the Ombudsman and her Office should play in respect of past deaths which resulted from the actions of a police officer, it was recognised the Ombudsman's Office also had a role in the project.

As further funding was not available, the allocation of the overall £34m was revised such that each of the organisations now confirmed as having a role would receive a proportionate amount. This led to some limited reallocation of funding in the financial year 2006/07.

The Government then set up arrangements to monitor closely the project's funding and expenditure, with representatives of the bodies involved meeting on a regular basis, to discuss financial issues. This might mean a request for easements and pressures to be offset, where possible, by the parties as they arose.

Mr Trevor Ringland, a then *Independent Member* of the Policing Board, on 10 November 2006 sent the Chairman a note on *'The Viability of Prosecution Based on Historical Enquiry: Observations of Counsel on Potential Evidential Difficulties'*. In his Introduction the author stated:

> *"At the outset, it is possible to identify three basic sources of difficulty likely to be encountered by the Enquiries Team:*
>
> > *1. There is the possible diminution of quality of evidence through the passage of time; for example, the actual recollection of witnesses will naturally be affected, changes will have taken place in the physical environment in which offences were committed and forensic evidence, if obtained, may not have been adequately preserved.*
> >
> > *2. In many cases evidence will simply be unavailable. Potentially material witnesses may have died or may prove impossible to trace. Forensic evidence, if not obtained at the time of the offence and preserved, will not readily be available to investigators. Further, confession evidence, which was a central feature of a large number of prosecutions for offences committed by paramilitaries in the course of the Troubles, is unlikely to be forthcoming.*
> >
> > *3. Any prosecutions that might arise from the fresh enquiries will be subject to the normal evidential and procedural rules, including for example the disclosure rules, the strict standards imposed on evidence of visual identification, the need for caution when relying on the evidence of potentially suspect witnesses, the hearsay rule and other rules of admissibility. Against the backdrop of such rules, the standard of proof beyond reasonable doubt imposed on the prosecution in criminal cases is an exacting one: it is perhaps trite to observe that the attainment of that standard becomes more formidable where the quality of the evidential material available to the prosecution has been diminished by the passage of time.'*

He concluded:

> *"This note has sought to highlight some of the evidential and*

> *procedural difficulties that are likely to arise from the work of the HET. It is not intended to suggest that prosecution for offences committed in past years is impossible. Indeed, as experience in other areas demonstrates, antiquity is not necessarily fatal to investigation and prosecution: one may refer, for example, to the successful prosecution of war criminals, convictions in cases of sexual abuse dating back many decades and the resurrection of seemingly dead lines of inquiry through the use of DNA technology. It is, however, submitted that any optimism engendered by the injection of resources into the process of historical inquiry needs to be tempered by the often harsh realities of proof in context of the criminal trial."*

In the presentation which he gave in November 2006 on the work of the PSNI's HET to a Sub-Committee of the Joint Committee on Justice, Equality, Defence and Women's Rights at the Oireachtas, Dublin, the Chief Constable said:

> *"I am very proud of our practical contribution to taking responsibility for what happened to police investigations during the Troubles, in the form of the HET. There were 3,268 deaths related to the security situation. In virtually every case, families have questions they would like answers to. In addition to these, tens of thousands of people were injured or traumatised, and still face significant challenges on a daily basis."*

He went on to acknowledge:

> *"There is not the capacity to deal with all these cases. Many very serious crimes will never be looked at again as the resources are just not available. We recognise that the likelihood of solving cases in a judicial sense is slight for a number of reasons. The primary aim of HET is to bring a measure of resolution to families. We have consciously shifted the focus to ensure that the driving force behind the team's effort will be to deliver the outcome the family seek rather than the more formal one-dimensional police* approach. *This approach is unique in UK policing."*

At the *public session* of the Policing Board held on 13 December 2006 in reply to a question from *Political Member* Alex Attwood (SDLP), the Chief Constable commented on the funding matter of *historical enquiries* as follows:

> *"In terms of the HET, we went to government and in fairness, government listened and very quickly provided us with £32m so that was the pot of money I had to do that bit of work. Currently, I am*

confident we can deliver pretty much what we want to deliver with that amount of cash and I spoke to David Cox only last Sunday and discussed it. At the minute we are moving on and we can deliver, I think, a reasonable amount with that money. If I think at any stage we need more, I am happy to go back and say we need that supplementing, because in terms of overall investment it is actually quite a small amount.

As far as the Ombudsman's Office is concerned, of course they have a statutory responsibility to investigate any of the crimes that we start dealing with where there is some suspicion that there was police involvement in that particular killing and I know she is very much switched on to that particular point and we do have conversations about it. What I would say is the money we bid for was the money for our bit of the business and if I lose much of that to try and fund another bit of the business then I am in difficulty, let's be very clear about that, so if my money is cut down just to fund the Ombudsman's investigations then I think we do have a difficulty.

I think it is also worth reflecting and I think there was a Parliamentary Question recently that secured an answer that suggested somewhere in the region of £18m has currently been spent on three public inquiries, so in that context I do not think £32m is a huge amount to deal with what we are trying to deal with for such a wide spectrum, but I do take a close personal interest in this. I supervise the HET directly myself and will continue to do so and if I do feel I am in difficulty I will come straight back to the Board.'

At the Policing Board meeting held on 13 December 2006 the Chairman informed Members that the Corporate Policy, Planning and Performance Committee at its meeting on 22 November 2006 had considered a paper on *'Dealing with the Past: Issues Aimed At Providing A Background to Facilitate Discussion'*. Among the issues noted or agreed were:

- The legislation governing the work of the Police Ombudsman (OPONI) permits investigations into incidents which occurred more than two years ago where certain criteria are met.
- The OPONI had identified a total of 75 'past' cases and the availability of resources to adequately investigate these had been identified as an issue by the office.
- The OPONI had also identified the non-cooperation of retired officers as

a barrier to effective investigation and ultimate closure for the families of victims in such cases.

- That the Policing Board could assist the PSNI with publicising the role of HET by inviting the Chief Constable and the HET top team to present in a public session at a future Board meeting.

The latter presentation relating to '"*dealing with the past" and the role of the police in this complex process*' was made in the *public session* of the Policing Board held on 5 July 2007. (NB On 31 May 2007 Sinn Fein took their seats on the Policing Board.) The Chief Constable began by '*painting a picture of all the agencies with all "parts of the past" which the PSNI is currently engaged with'* to which he added the Coroner (44 additional cases overall). He then moved to the HET, its role, its progress and its overall costs, including covering post-Good Friday Agreement cases, which fell outside the ambit of the HET. He also covered the costs and pressures around inquiries. The Chief Constable and his senior team were then questioned by Board Members.

On 5 July 2007 the NIO Minister Paul Goggins wrote to the Policing Board as follows:

> *"I am writing in response to your letters about the proposed stocktake of the HET as well as funding issues arising from the recommendations contained in the Police Ombudsman's report into the murder of Raymond McCord Jnr. I apologise for the delay.*
>
> *The Historic Enquiries Team is a unique project. I remain extremely supportive of their efforts to provide information, explanation and, where appropriate investigation in relation to the many deaths which occurred during the Troubles for which no full account has been given. Dealing with the past in a way that fully respects the needs of victims and their families while at the same time ensuring that issues of the past do not unduly dominate the present is an issue of increasing concern to all of us, and I know the Board is particularly interested in how this can be achieved.*
>
> *I am confident that the recently established panel on the past represents the most constructive way forward in attempting to address many of these issues. While I look forward to reading their report and recommendations, the panel is not expected to complete its work until next year. In the immediate future, therefore, it is important that we proceed with the proposed HET stocktake in order*

to establish how many cases have been dealt with so far, and at what cost; and what the likely timescale is for completion of the work. I have discussed this idea with both the Chief Constable and the Police Ombudsman and it is hoped to agree terms of reference with the organisations involved in the project and begin the stocktake in the near future. I will of course ensure the Policing Board is kept fully informed of progress.

£34 million has been allocated to the work of HET. In suggesting that we take stock of how the HET project is progressing I am, however, conscious of the extension of the remit of HET to address a number of issues arising from the Police Ombudsman's report into the murder of Raymond McCord Jnr and the possible financial and operational impact caused by the investigations. I am aware that the HET paper presented to the Policing Board indicated that these new investigations would cost an additional £1.52m per annum.'

At the 22 March 2007 Board meeting in 'matters arising' from the minutes of the previous meeting, the Chairman reminded Members that during questions to the Chief Constable there had been a discussion regarding HET funding issues arising from the OPONI report of the investigation of the murder of Raymond McCord Jnr (the Ballast Report). He advised Members that he had been informed by the NIO in a letter dated 20 February 2007 that the Minister of State for Northern Ireland, Paul Goggins, considered that a review of how the HET was progressing in financial and general terms should be initiated. The Chairman wrote to the Minister seeking clarification of his *'intentions in respect of the more "general terms" [he] had in mind.'*

On 4 July 2007 the NIO Minister Paul Goggins, wrote to the Chairman in respect of *'the HET, the investigation of cases arising from the OPONI's report into the murder of Raymond McCord Jnr, and the proposed stocktake'* as follows:

"Unfortunately, given the current financial pressures, I do not envisage being in a position to make available any specific additional resources for this purpose.

I would be happy to discuss further when we next meet."

At the meeting of the Policing Board held on 6 September 2007 the following exchanges took place in respect of the HET:

'Chairman, Professor Sir Desmond Rea:

"One issue that was raised earlier this morning Chief Constable,

related to the publicity in recent weeks in respect of the HET and particular, in respect of the financing of the HET........".

Chief Constable, Sir Hugh Orde:

"... I met with the Minister yesterday, with Alistair Finlay my ACC Crime Support, and I am happy to report that we had a conversation around the funding to date and we are happy that we have that money, but more importantly, the money is secured to ensure the future of the HET is safe."

Assistant Chief Constable, Mr Alistair Finlay:

"Thank you. We have had very positive meetings with NIO officials. There was confusion about last year's budget and where that actually came from and how it was accounted for and that is down to accounting practices it would appear. However, it is quite clear what budget we have for the current financial year and we have engaged in a process with the NIO around future meetings which will identify funding needs for forthcoming years so this ambiguity does not arise in the future."

The Policing Board at its meeting on 1 November 2007 considered correspondence dated 17 October 2007 from the NIO Policing Division regarding the *HET stocktake*. Attached to the letter were the following terms of reference as agreed with the PSNI:

'HET STOCKTAKE TERMS OF REFERENCE:
To consider how best to continue to deliver the objectives of the HET project taking into account the experience/knowledge gained to date and the existing budgetary constraints.

HET STOCKTAKE – OBJECTIVES

- *to critically analyse the current budget with the aim of: (a) reaching an assessment of the probable budgetary requirements to complete the task as currently scoped and (b) consider options that could allow the task to be completed within the current budget allocation;*
- *to explore the possibilities of adopting additional practical working arrangements that will as far as possible ensure that as many cases as possible continue to be resolved in the shortest possible timescale;*

- *to agree budgets for 2008/09-2010/11; and*
- *to consider if/how the organisations involved in HET might manage resources more effectively.'*

The letter added:

> *'[We] will be taking forward the stocktake shortly. [We] will continue to keep you informed of progress.'*

Members, having discussed the work and finances of the HET and the timing of the *stocktake*, agreed that the Chairman should write to the Minister of State for Northern Ireland, Paul Goggins, recommending that the *stocktake* be postponed until the Consultative Group on the Past had presented its findings; the Chairman did so on 14 November 2007 and received the following reply, dated 10 January 2008, from Minister Goggins:

> *"Thank you for your letter of 14 November concerning the HET Stocktake Terms of Reference.*
>
> *I note your concern in relation to the potential impact of the deliberations by the Consultative Group on the Past on the work of the HET. However, I feel that it is important that we continue with the* **stocktake** *as it will deal with a number of immediate financial and administrative issues, and any deferment of the stocktake is likely to have a negative impact on the HET project.*
>
> *Any recommendations of the Consultative Group on the Past that might impact on the HET project will of course be considered as part of our broader response to the Group's report. The work carried out as part of the stocktake should prove beneficial in this regard.*
>
> *In recognition of the Board's interest in the* **stocktake**, *I have asked my officials to ensure that the Board is kept fully informed of its progress.'*

In a written reply to a question to the PSNI at the Policing Board meeting held on 6 December 2007 from *Political Member* David Simpson (DUP), the Chief Constable provided the following information:

- The HET was established to examine all deaths attributed to the Troubles from January 1969 to the Good Friday Agreement in 1998; this equates to 3,268 deaths from 2,516 incidents (NB The HET assign cases per incident).
- The HET is also undertaking the PSNI response to the OPONI report into the death of Raymond McCord Jnr, a linked series of 29 additional investigations.

- The HET allocates 40 operations per week period into its processes of Assessment, Review, Focussed Investigation and Resolution.

At the Policing Board meeting held on 5 June 2008, *Political Member* David Simpson (DUP) asked the Chief Constable the following questions about the HET:

- *"What impact have the high levels of resignation from the HET had on its on-going work?*
- *How many cases have passed the anticipated completion date?"*

To the first question the Chief Constable replied as follows:

> *"The HET accepted from the beginning that, in order to attain the level of independence required to achieve family and wider community engagement, a large number of personnel would need to be recruited from outside of Northern Ireland. Our current establishment is made up of 84% agency staff and 16% a mix of PSNI, seconded officers and consultants. Currently, the team employ 100 people from outside Northern Ireland who fly in on a Monday and out on a Friday. A team made up of people from many different police services throughout the UK, away from colleagues, organisations they know and family and friends. Between 1 April 2007 and 31 March 2008 the HET establishment grew by 29%. The attrition rate for 07/08 was 38%. Due to the nature of the work and the circumstances, which require staff to live away from their families during the week, the HET have always expected that this would limit the time many employees remain with the team.*
>
> *It is also important to note that in April 2006 the HET employed 13 seconded police staff. Those secondments naturally ended and the officers returned to force. Police forces (particularly in the current climate) can only afford to have officers seconded for limited periods. At the time, the total size of the HET was only 95 so the seconded officers represented a good percentage of that (14% compared with 6% in April 2007).*
>
> *Overall the HET, which began work in January 2006, has a very committed team, 22% have stayed over two years, and just over 50% have been here between one and two years. We have to accept that the nature of the work is also difficult; and that our staff are dealing with many sad and complex cases on a daily basis.*

There may be an impact on work rate, but not unduly. That is a part of this kind of initiative; senior management has remained largely consistent, which is useful."

In respect of the second question the Chief Constable said:

"The reality around the work of the team is that in the first two years:

- *An entirely new process has been created and has had to evolve.*
- *Funding secured.*
- *Team and premises established.*
- *Exhibits, files gathered – an enormous task and work has begun on cases.*
- *The team have completed 363 reviews and currently have 1,107 cases open.*
- *Relationships built with many and diverse groups who consult and advise, not to mention the 713 families HET have been working with to date."*

In late July 2008 former Police Ombudsman, Dame Nuala O'Loan, called for a merger of the HET and the Police Ombudsman's office.

"There needs to be a single unit comprising the HET and historic investigations from the Police Ombudsman,' she said …

'It would be more cost effective because they would not both be investigating the same cases, on occasion in parallel, which is very difficult. …

It would be independent of the PSNI and RUC – which would answer a lot of the problems some relatives currently have.

Because you would have one organisation, it would reduce the administrative cost and would be a case-limited function.

I think there needs to be a single unit and I think the funding needs to be proportionate to the problem.'

[Contrasting the hundreds of millions of pounds already paid out to police officers retiring under reforms of the RUC, she said,] *'If we can spend that on Patten severance then I think government should be able to find the money to investigate these past cases.'*

Later Mr Al Hutchinson, Dame Nuala O'Loan's successor, said that such a merger should be considered. Mr Dave Cox, Head of the HET, on 5 August 2008 stated that there should be closer working.

At the Policing Board meeting of 2 October 2008 the Chairman, under 'Publications', said that the following publication had been received:

> Lundy, Patricia; *Can the Past be Policed? Lessons from the Historical Enquiries Team, Northern Ireland (Draft)*

In her 'Introduction' Dr Lundy stated;

> *"This article explores how societies in transition might address victims' quest for "the truth", or more specifically micro level information. It does this by using a case study of the Historical Enquiries Team (HET) established by the Police Service of Northern Ireland (PSNI). The HET is a unique attempt by a police service in a society undergoing transition to "police the past". In September 2005 the Chief Constable of the PSNI, Sir Hugh Orde, granted permission to conduct the research and wide and unfettered access to the HET was permitted. It is notable that in the context of Northern Ireland this was unprecedented access to policing. The article therefore offers a unique insight into a unique process...."*

Under '*Part 4: Structural Impediments, Obstacles and Constraints'* and in particular *'Staffing and Independence'*, Dr Lundy concluded,

> *"From a detailed analysis of various cross-referenced sources, and over two years observation of the HET, the research found that each phase of the HET CARIR process (Collection, Assessment, Review, Investigation, Resolution) has involvement by former long serving RUC officers and cannot be described as having the requisite degree of independence as benchmarked by Brecknell (in Brecknell v the United Kingdom) and required by the ECHR."*

In respect of *the collection phase* she added,

> *'The manner in which [this] phase is conducted casts doubt upon the integrity of the process and the very foundation on which the HET is built.'*

At the meeting of the Policing Board held on 4 December 2008 the Chairperson of the Board's Human Rights and Professional Standards Committee highlighted that the Chief Constable, Assistant Chief Constable Jones, the HET Director, Dave Cox, and Deputy Director Phil James had attended the Committee's meeting on 12 November 2008 and had briefed the Committee on Dr Lundy's article. The Chief Constable had advised the Committee that,

> *'Since the article was still in draft form, he was disappointed that it had appeared on the internet. He expressed disappointment on the content of the paper.'*

In 2012 the Minister of Justice for Northern Ireland commissioned Her Majesty's Inspectorate of Constabulary to inspect the role and function of the PSNI HET with (in summary) the following Terms of Reference (ToR) :

- ToR 1. Does the HET's approach conform to current policing standards and practices?
- ToR 2 Does the HET adopt a consistent approach to all cases?
- ToR 3 Is the HET's approach to cases with State involvement compliant with European Convention on Human Rights and Fundamental Freedoms (ECHR)?

HMIC published its report on 9 July 2013:
In respect of ToR 1, HMIC concluded: *"Our findings indicate an unacceptable large range where the HET's approach does not conform to current policing standards and practices."*

In respect to ToR 2, HMIC concluded: *"Our inspection found that the HET, as a matter of policy, treats deaths where there was State involvement differently from those cases where there is no State involvement. State involvement cases appeared to be treated less rigorously."*

In respect to ToR 3, HMIC concluded: "*[Our] conclusions lead us to consider that the HET's approach to State involvement cases is inconsistent with the United Kingdom's obligations under Article 2 EHCR..... In addition the deployment of former RUC and PSNI officers in State involvement cases gives rise to the view that the process lacks independence."*

On 30 September 2013 Chief Constable Matt Baggott announced that Chief Superintendent Tina Barnett would replace Commander Dave Cox as Leader of the HET; there was to be a handover period of two weeks.

With respect to NIAC's report into policing and criminal justice in Northern Ireland, '*The Cost of Policing the Past',* as published in early July 2008, the Policing Board's Corporate Policy Committee at its meeting on 18 September 2008 received a background note containing the following summary of the background to the NIAC's report and the key points identified by it:

*'1. **Background***
The report examines whether the cost of "policing the past" is compromising the PSNI and the Police Ombudsman's Office in carrying out their functions. The report recommends alternative ways for the Historical Enquiries Team (HET) to prioritise case-load in order to manage funding more effectively. Significant additional funding would be required to maintain the HET's current approach. The report also recommends that a mid-term review is conducted to establish the costs and benefits of continuing with the HET's present methods.

The first phase of the inquiry focussed on two specific areas of concern:

- *The financial and operating consequences of the Police Service of Northern Ireland of servicing the various "historic inquiries" into past events in Northern Ireland.*
- *The effect on the ability of the Police Service of Northern Ireland to bring accused persons to trial of provisions in the Public Inquiries Act 2005 and in other legislation requiring the police to divulge information which might identify a covert source.*

*2. **Detail***
Key points identified by the report:

- *All cases are automatically reviewed by HET but it is recommended that alternative ways of prioritising cases are identified so that resources can be focussed on those cases where the next of kin of the deceased specifically request it or where the existence of forensics or other exhibits provides investigative opportunities which could contribute to a successful prosecution case.*
- *A mid-term project review should be conducted to establish the costs and benefits of continuing with the HET in its current form and identifying ways in which the prioritisation of cases could be adjusted so that the project can be completed within budget.*
- *The findings of the review should be published.*
- *The HET should be managed by an independent agency instead of PSNI. This would allow the PSNI to return to its core functions.*
- *The extension of the Ombudsman's remit to include*

historic cases is having a negative effect on the efficiency of the Office, but the report does not wish to make any recommendation on this until the conclusions of the Eames/ Bradley Group are available.

- *The PSNI has expressed specific concerns about the inquiries' information management procedures – these concerns should be included in the Government's review of inquiry information management procedures and if not there, then in a further review as a matter of urgency.*
- *The NIO should take further steps to control the costs of Northern Ireland's statutory inquiries and that future inquiries should only be established if agreed by the Northern Ireland Assembly.*
- *An information management code of conduct should be drawn up by the coroner, after consultation with the appropriate agencies, to protect sensitive information provided to him as part of the inquest process, and that any public disclosure of such information is made in accordance with the coroner's obligations under ECHR Article 2.*
- *The impact of the inquests on the PSNI's resources and any consequential effect on current policing capacity is reviewed during 2009 and the budget revised accordingly.'*

The Policing Board's response to NIAC's first specific area of concern as agreed at the former's Corporate Policy, Planning and Performance Committee on 17 January 2008 was:

> *"It is the view of the Board that the effectiveness and efficiency of the PSNI in preventing and detecting crime should not be compromised by dealing with the various commitments to historical inquiries.*
>
> *It is the responsibility of Government to ensure that the PSNI be provided with adequate funding to deal with* ***policing the past****, and the Board is committed to ensuring Government deliver the necessary funding for the PSNI in this area.*
>
> *A consensus view could not be reached on the second specific area of concern of the Committee Inquiry and therefore the Board did not respond on this point. It was agreed that members would respond separately on a party political or individual basis."*

The Corporate Policy, Planning and Performance Committee on 18 September 2008, having considered the NIAC's report, responded accordingly.

On 18 December 2008 the Chairman of the Policing Board wrote to the Chief Constable as follows:

> *"HISTORICAL ENQUIRIES TEAM FUNDING*
> *I write to express on behalf of the Board surprise and disappointment on the handling of the news that the HET are to make staff redundant from April 2009.*
>
> *This news started to break immediately following the Board meeting on 4 December 2008 during which a considerable amount of time was devoted to the consideration of the current financial difficulties facing the PSNI. At no stage did the PSNI mention that such an announcement was imminent. The Board was disappointed to find out about this matter through third parties and the media. The situation was all the more surprising in the context of the many discussions in recent weeks on the financial issues.*
> *The Board would welcome an explanation as to why it was not briefed on this issue on 4 December 2008 at its meeting."*

And he received the following reply from the Chief Constable dated 13 January 2009:

> *"I note the issues you raise, however I think that an element of confusion may have arisen in the media coverage about resources allocated to the Historical Enquiries Team (HET).*
>
> *It is not my intention to make any staff attached to HET redundant. The project is a bespoke piece of work, which is separately funded by the Northern Ireland Office (NIO) with a ring-fenced budget of £34m. (the Legacy Fund), established by the NIO in 2005 and scheduled to be apportioned on a yearly basis for six years up to 2011.*
>
> *As with any project, it has a definitive time scale attached to it and personnel are employed on a temporary basis. The staff members are supplied by a number of Employment Agencies, including Grafton and Servoca. Conditions of employment are governed by a contract drawn up under the national framework that covers the use of agency workers to support police forces.*
>
> *The use of agency staff provides the flexibility to deploy qualified and*

experienced investigators, and numbers of staff engaged can vary according to needs and requirements. This is an ideal arrangement for a project such as HET.

In the financial year 2008/2009, the NIO allowed HET to draw upon additional funding to underpin some particularly complex inquiries that it was engaged in (most notably, OPONI Operation Ballast cases). It also allowed HET to re-structure around a new investigative approach, recruiting experienced senior investigating officers to command smaller teams. The NIO advanced this money because their assessment of future developments around the Eames/Bradley proposals indicated that a new approach might be introduced before the end of the Legacy Fund time scale of 2011 was reached.

On 5 November 2008 the NIO informed us that the promised additional funding (£1.5m) would not now be available because of the deterioration in the overall economic climate. This generated significant public concern and at the beginning of December the NIO reversed this decision.

At the same time as this was unfolding, HET was in negotiation with the NIO over the budget for the financial year 2009/2010. This was set by the NIO at £5.9m., which was the notional sum for that year agreed at the outset of the project. However, HET was informed that, for this year, there was no potential for flexibility because of the overall economic situation and pressure on public finances.

This is an entirely separate issue from the previous budget pressure, and the new HET structure has built on its experiences to introduce smaller, more professional teams that are intended to deliver an increased number of case reviews, whilst meeting the strict public funding requirements.

HET has made no formal announcements about the re-structuring process involved, which is an internal re-profiling and part of a continuing evolutionary process. The new HET model will need fewer posts, a total of 120 as opposed to the existing 190.

The re-structuring will not commence until mid-January 2009 and will not become effective until 1 April. This being a period in which the normal consultative mechanisms would have taken place and both the Board and key stakeholders made aware of the changes.

However, the senior management had undertaken to keep staff apprised of developments throughout, and has worked closely with the supplying agencies to allow them to plan for the supply of staff required. An internal memo, intended to keep staff informed of developments and selection processes, was leaked to the media on the afternoon of 4 December 2008. The media immediately aligned it with an existing story about police budgets and linked back to previous concerns over the 2008 budget shortfall.

Although this was an unauthorised leak, HET issued a press line, intended to re-assure the public and families with whom it is engaged, that operational commitment would not be affected. This was carried in the newspapers the following day. HET also immediately engaged directly with a number of key partners to try and keep this issue in a proper perspective. Unfortunately, at that time the Policing Board was already in session.

I can categorically state that no announcement was made or planned about HET funding. In addition, staff will not be made redundant, although fewer temporary posts will be required after April 2009. It is clear that the unauthorised leak of this internal memo has resulted in media attention that subsequently linked the issue to previous concerns and other financial pressures facing HET.

I hope that this will go some way to allay the concerns you have expressed. HET continues to represent an excellent investment, both in respect of bringing answers to families, to date 509 cases have been reviewed with 808 families engaged and 5,686 questions recorded, and in financial terms, contrasted with the tens of millions of pounds expended on other processes that have yet to offer a single answer to any party."

At the *public session* of the Policing Board meeting held on 4 December 2008 in reply to the following question from *Political Member* Ian Paisley Jnr:

"What [Chief Constable] is [your] view regarding the prospect that the HET may become subsumed within a commission based upon any proposals made by the Consultative Group on the Past?"

The Chief Constable's (written) response was as follows:

"[I am] already on record as saying that the HET is offering something of real value to many hundreds of families. The unique process has been pioneered in consultation with families of victims and

groups working in this field, and it is tailored to their needs. HET is working, it is delivering to real people and is a team of which we can justifiably be proud. From the outset I viewed the work of the HET as being a component, one key part of, the wider societal response to issues arising from the past. We could not be, and did not set out to be, "everything" in this regard. There may be benefits in bringing all the mechanisms which currently look at these important and very sensitive issues under the umbrella of some type of new commission, in the expectation that any new body will bring more, not less, to the assistance of these families. The HET has been structured around thoroughness, fairness and consistency. There has been a great deal of learning and development, relationships have been built, and this valuable experience should not be lost. Consultations are on-going with the Consultation group on the Past. At this stage, if the families we are working for continue to be given the best possible assistance, under those circumstances I would not oppose the transfer of the Historical Enquiries Team to another body."

As at 5 February 2009 the HET had completed over 500 'reviews' and delivered case reports to 200 families. Over the first four years of its existence the HET had cost over £21m.

It is the understanding of the authors that the 'stocktake' on the HET was not completed.

Chapter Four

Holding The Past In A Healthy Balance With The Future

4.1 Where We Are

As pointed out at the beginning of this short book there were certain matters/ issues which motivated the Chairman to initiate (repeatedly) a debate on *Dealing With Northern Ireland's Troubled Past.* These included:

- In bringing the Northern Ireland Troubles to an end there have been and are two processes in play: one **the *political process*** and the other **the *peace process***. The ***political process*** and its parameters are well known and relatively speaking little controversy is attached to them. The latter, however, cannot be said of ***the peace process***; it is critical that it moves constructively and steadily towards completion.
- Of the 3,739 deaths perpetrated in the Troubles some 2,000 were estimated by the Chief Constable Hugh Orde as being unsolved and should be re-investigated. However, since he believed that to do so within the PSNI's then existing budget and staffing would distract from current policing needs and the pursuit of the modernising agenda of The Report Of The Independent Commission On Policing For Northern Ireland, he argued successfully to the NIO for the setting up of the HET. It was also a matter of the HET being, and being seen to be, independent and fully skilled for the task and the HMIC Report published in July 2013 has raised questions about both.
- The accuracy of Sir Hugh Orde's statement of 10 June 2005 – referred to above – cannot be doubted, viz:

  > *"… demands for public inquiries become the order of the day, with a focus on State collusion and conspiracy. This one-dimensional approach fails to acknowledge the sheer scale of the miserable history, and allows a hierarchy of death to be created where some victims are deemed more important than others. In statistical terms, it is a matter of fact that the majority of re-investigations and enquiries currently underway are focussed on victims of alleged State involvement in the murder in a context where the majority of deaths and injuries resulted from the actions of paramilitary*

> *organisations. The impact on other victims is substantial. They feel disenfranchised, and do not see the State pursuing their loved ones' killers with matching vigour. ..."*

(NB Republican paramilitaries killed approximately six times as many persons as did Security personnel and Loyalist paramilitaries killed approximately three times as many persons as did Security personnel.) Sir Hugh Orde could have added '... and lead to an even more divided society'.

- On the back of the Police Ombudsman's Report on the Omagh bombing and Cory's Report on Patrick Finucane, there have been calls for public inquiries. Indeed the Labour Party, if elected to power, have committed to one for the latter. But in respect of the Omagh call, why not the Enniskillen bombing or indeed the Claudy bombing? Besides the costs, would not an inquiry into the latter open up a sectarian can of worms and lead to an even more divided society? As to a public inquiry for Patrick Finucane, see below.
- As *The Financial Times* put it when commenting on the Saville Report on 15 June 2010:

> *"The Saville inquiry, meanwhile, has left significant loose ends. A notable one is whether prosecutions should be brought against those soldiers whom the judge came close to accusing of unlawful killing and perjury.*
>
> *The idea of plunging into new legal thickets is daunting, especially since it might well prove hard to convert Lord Saville's findings into convictions against individuals. And few want to pursue soldiers, even if they were guilty of serious wrongdoing, when virtually all IRA members convicted of terrorist offences were long ago set free as part of the peace process. Unionists are opposed to prosecutions. Most nationalists are too, considering that, with the pronouncements of the judge and the prime minister, truth has been told and honour satisfied."*

Likewise it is in no-one's interest that charges to do with terrorism about something in the distant past should hypothetically be placed at the door of say, a current Member of the Northern Ireland Executive or of the Policing Board.

4.2 Where Now?

The reader will have noted that the Chairman of the Northern Ireland Policing Board sought and received the permission of Policing Board Members on 17 June 2003 to read to them a paper entitled *'Seeking to Hold the Past in a Healthy Balance with the Future'*. The Vice-Chairman Denis Bradley endorsed it and so too later did Chief Constable Hugh Orde. The subject was raised again on 3 March 2004 and on 1 December 2004. During the later discussion,

> *'Whilst Members agreed that the general debate on the issue of dealing with Northern Ireland's past should be driven by others outside the policing environment, Members also agreed that there was a need for further debate within the Board.'*

On 3 February 2005 it was agreed that a group of Members should consider the issue. On 21 April 2005 it was further agreed that a response to the NIAC's report on *'Ways of Dealing with the Past'* be considered at a future meeting; this happened on 2 June 2005, where it was agreed that no further action should be taken by the Board at present. At the Board meeting held on 30 June 2005 *'the consensus view was that issues concerning dealing with the past would be taken forward by Government and the political parties, rather than the Board.'* On 15 May 2006 the Chairman wrote to the Minister of State Paul Goggins enclosing a copy of Annex A to this chapter and drawing to his attention the recommendation under the *'Way Forward'*. This appears to have played a significant part in the process leading to the formation by the then Secretary of State Peter Hain of the *'Independent Consultative Group on the Past'* (Eames/Bradley). We noted above that the latter's report and recommendations disappeared without trace, a fate it did not deserve, arguably a judgement on our political class and on us as a people. But dealing with our 'past' will not go away.

On 8 August 2007 the Chairman was invited to join a *'West Belfast Talkback'* panel at the West Belfast Festival. The other members of the panel were Ms Caitriona Ruane (Sinn Fein), Mr Edwin Poots (DUP) and Mr Eoghan Harris (*Sunday Independent*). The first question was addressed to the Chairman:

> *'Professor Rea, I am Patrick Finucane's son. Your views on "dealing with the past" are well known but where do they leave me and my family?'*

In reply the Chairman referred to the paper which is at Annex A to this book and is in the names of Denis Bradley and Hugh Orde as well as his own name.

However, he went further, identifying in his argument, where he was doing so:

> *"First, I sympathise with you, your mother and your family in the death of your father but everywhere I go in Northern Ireland I meet similar pain, be it the relatives of the Omagh bombing or RUC or PSNI widows.'*

In respect of individuals he had in mind a letter dated June 2005, which he had received from two sisters, Denise Jardin Lowry and Sylvia Jardin, which is published here with permission:

> *'Our father, Andrew Jardin of White Gables, Hannahstown, Belfast, was murdered on 23 December 1970 in his home, five days after his 65th birthday. He had lived at White Gables, Hannahstown, since he was a child.*
>
> *This completely destroyed our family and our mother never recovered from it.*
>
> *We would like to know if the perpetrators of this crime were ever discovered and what the situation is at present, as it will be 35 years this coming December and we have never been given any information regarding the outcome of the case.*
>
> *There are many murders being examined at present, which took place relatively recently, many of them high profile cases. To us our father's murder is a 'high profile' case.*
>
> *The minister, at his funeral in Woodvale Presbyterian Church, described our father as a church-going, generous man who believed in justice, freedom and truth. He had served king and country during the Second World War.*
>
> *He was Managing Director of Workman Limited, a Director of Workman Forth & Jardin and Managing Director of the Black Mountain Quarry near his home. He employed both Catholics and Protestants in all branches of the firm.*
>
> *We would appreciate any assistance you could give us in our search for information."*

Much more recently, in respect again of an individual killing we would add this, through the words of Mark Heaney in the *Irish Times* of 23 February 2013. Writing about an RTE radio documentary *'A Knock on the Door'*, he told about the fatally botched IRA kidnapping in 1973 of German industrialist

Thomas Niedermayer through the prism of his bereft family. *'Having eventually moved back to Germany, his [widow] returned to Ireland in 1990, booked into a hotel in Bray, Co. Wicklow, and walked into the sea'*. Later his two daughters committed suicide.

As far as the authors are concerned there is no hierarchy of death.

In his response to Mr Finucane the Chairman continued.... . *Second, I have bought into the peace process on Sinn Fein's terms, which I understand to be – and correct me if I am wrong – Sinn Fein has argued that its paramilitary wing, viz PIRA:*

- *was an army not terrorists,*
- *was engaged in a war and,*
- *since the Troubles was a war, the prisoners of war should be released.*

(NB The Chairman was referring to Annex B, Prisoners, in the 10 April 1998 Belfast Agreement: 1. "Both Governments will put in place mechanisms to provide for an accelerated programme for the release of prisoners ... 2. Prisoners affiliated to organisations, which have not established or are not maintaining a complete and unequivocal ceasefire will not benefit from the arrangements"... etc etc ....)

For the Chairman this meant that Sinn Fein members elected to the Northern Ireland Assembly, or indeed Progressive Unionist Party members if elected to the Northern Ireland Assembly, should – regardless of record and depending on the size of their membership – be Members of the Policing Board or the Northern Ireland Assembly's Executive.

The Chairman then put to the audience – and the audience included the Leader of Sinn Fein, Gerry Adams – the question, "*Does this not mean that both Governments have accepted Sinn Fein's argument?*" No-one voiced their disagreement.

Third, he added;

'In a war nasty things happen on both sides. I do not challenge that collusion took place. Whilst you can argue that more can be expected from a State (Article 2 of the European Convention on Human Rights), it would seem disingenuous to do so, if as Sinn Fein has argued, and it has been implicitly accepted by both Governments that they were engaged in a war, and not in terrorism. Accordingly:

- *as of, say, the Belfast Agreement, the slate should be wiped clean, and our society and policing should look to the future;*

- *the release of prisoners should be extended to an amnesty for all;*
- *there should be no more inquiries; and*
- *our concern as a society should be for the victims at their point of need.*

To the above we would add:

- Northern Ireland should draw a line in a 'national' act of public contrition;
- That the above programme should be ratified in a Northern Ireland referendum.

There is the separate, but clearly related, issue of the continuing work of the Historical Enquiries Team and the reinvestigation of deaths during the Troubles up to April 1998. The HET has been a unique experiment in the context of international policing – a Northern Ireland solution to a Northern Ireland problem. Given its funding constraints and despite recent criticism- see below- in many ways, it has been successful. While very few of the reinvestigations so far completed have led to prosecutions, undoubtedly much comfort has been provided to the relatives of victims in terms of information that was not made available to them at the time of death.

But, as with the costs associated with public inquiries, and contrary to the view expressed by Hugh Orde in 2006, the original six-year budget of £34m has proved very inadequate. Eight years or so after it was set up, the HET has so far tackled only around one half of all the identified cases.

Second, as not originally foreseen, when the HET was established, there have also proved to be issues relating to the currency of its professional expertise. As a comparatively small unit, made up largely of retired and seconded officers from outside Northern Ireland, inevitably their skill set and ability to tap into all the latest technical resources are limited. This led to the decision to bring HET more closely into the PSNI structure, with the clear objective of obtaining the best outcome for the relatives in the individual cases.

In addition, its work has been challenged by the issues of superintendence and the relationship with the Police Ombudsman. Indeed, although it is not within the scope of this book, the work of the Ombudsman's Office itself in investigating historic cases has been controversial, and proved to be one of the factors that led to Al Hutchinson's leaving the post when he did.

Superintendence is an interesting point. One of the authors, being involved in the discussions between the Northern Ireland Office and Hugh Orde when the latter's initial proposals for what became the HET were brought forward, argued unsuccessfully for an independent element. Such a role would have covered not just the accountability function, as with the Policing Board, but also a more explicitly outward-facing dimension, intended to assist the staff of the HET in their public liaison work. The Policing Board formally had responsibility, as has been demonstrated earlier in this book, although this was in practice carried out with a fairly light touch. The Northern Ireland Affairs Committee report recommended that the HET should be managed by an independent agency rather than the PSNI, and Sir Hugh Orde wrote to the Policing Board in late 2008 putting on the record that he would not oppose the transfer of the HET to another body. In practice, no such change was made.

In the summer of 2013, a further issue arose, in relation to the legal approach being adopted by the HET towards the investigation of cases where the primary responsibility for the death was attributed to the Army.

The question of reinvestigation of the remaining cases, should, we believe, be included within the spirit of the way forward set out above.

Finally, we would recall that the Northern Ireland Affairs Committee's Interim Report *Ways of Dealing with Northern Ireland's Past*, published in April 2005, presciently had this to say about the plight of relatives of the "disappeared":

> *'Until those who have information come forward to enable the remains outstanding to be recovered, it will in our view be impossible for Northern Ireland to move forward fully.'*

We agree.

Annex A

SEEKING TO HOLD THE PAST IN A HEALTHY BALANCE WITH THE FUTURE

1. Introduction

For some time we have been concerned about 'Dealing with the Past in Northern Ireland'. There is no doubt this is an extremely sensitive issue which provokes many emotions; but one which we believe needs addressed in a way which seeks to hold the past in a healthy balance with the future.

We have all in some way, previously publicly expressed our personal views on this subject. This paper is designed to focus minds on how this subject can best be dealt with; and also on issues which are inextricably linked to dealing with this subject.

This document also formed the basis of a submission to the Northern Ireland Affairs Committee (NIAC) which conducted an Inquiry into *'Ways of Dealing with Northern Ireland's Past'.* In April 2005 the NIAC published an Interim Report of this Inquiry entitled 'Victims and Survivors' and its recommendations are relevant reading when considering options for the way forward.

2. Background

David Bolton in a recent article posed the following question:

'To what degree is progress dependent on addressing the past?'

Which he answered as follows:

> *'I am reminded of John Paul Lederach's dictum: "remember and change where the past is held in healthy balance with the future" and how people should remember in helpful and creative ways while engaging in positive change. We can either sweep the past under the carpet or engage in endless and divisive forensic purity. A man whose daughter died in the Oklahoma bombing comes to mind. He reached a pivotal moment in his grief when he enquired of himself:*
>
> > *"What would it take to enable me to be reconciled to my loss and to inhabit the future, for my own personal peace of mind?"'*
>
> *In the Troubles some 3,366 people have been killed, of those 1,525 were Catholics and 1,250 Protestants. 302 police*

officers were killed and over 9,000 police officers were injured, as were 46,753 lay people.

Many to this day mourn their dead. Many to this day are bruised and hurt. Too many cases are unresolved and relatives left without closure. Some families who believe, rightly or wrongly, that the killing of their relatives involved collusion with the security forces wanted and want public inquiries. Some families simply want to forget.

For our collective good maybe we need to ask ourselves the same question as that posed by the man whose daughter died in the Oklahoma bombing and thereafter agree on a 'good enough' way of settling the past.'

It would seem a sensible approach:

- To learn from the past in a positive way;
- To understand the present; and
- To provide for the future in such a way that we do not regress to the past.

3. **Policing Context**

Within the new policing arrangements there is an overwhelming desire to move forward and police the future. That is not to say that past unresolved cases are not worthy of police time and effort.

There is a desire to work within the current legislative framework and the European Convention on Human Rights (ECHR) context and a desire for justice; but from a practical perspective Patten's 7,500 officers did not take account of a need to police the past to the extent that is now becoming evident and indeed being demanded from some quarters.

The potential for many re-investigations (Cory and Police Ombudsman investigation of past cases; in excess of 2,300 unsolved killings, the pressure on the Chief Constable to investigate the murders of policemen and women) has obvious resource implications for the investigative capacity of the Police Service of Northern Ireland (PSNI) – an area that already has a shortage. Hence the need for Section 23 of the Police (Northern Ireland) Act 2003 and provision for the appointment (outside of 50:50) of constables with special policing skills.

A team of officers was established within Crime Operations Department in 2004 to deal solely with the investigation of past unsolved murders. Government has also recently announced £32m of funding for PSNI to establish a new unit which is now operating, staffed with suitably qualified investigators to work on all unresolved deaths.

The question has to be asked though, is the desire for justice within the gift of PSNI to deliver? – what do the families of the victims want? Will the new Victims Commissioner, likely to take up appointment soon, be able to help us answer some of these questions?

4. **Societal Context**

There have been two processes running concurrently which have sought to address the Northern Ireland conflict:

- First, the peace process; and
- Secondly, the political process.

The parameters of the latter are well known and are not the purport of this brief paper. Sinn Fein have argued that their paramilitary wing – namely the Provisional IRA:

- Was an army, not terrorists;
- Was engaged in a war, and since it was a war the prisoners of war should be released.

By releasing the prisoners does this mean that the British Government has *implicitly* recognised Sinn Fein's argument?

Similarly, on the Loyalist side, prisoners have been released in accordance with the terms of the early release scheme.

Let us envisage a scenario where we have, firstly devolution in Northern Ireland up and running again with a cross-party executive including Sinn Fein.

Then, secondly, we have the five inquiries recommended by Peter Cory QC. Let us remember that his terms of reference were as follows:

> *'To conduct a thorough investigation into allegations of collusion by the security forces in six particular cases to which the two governments committed themselves following the discussions with the Northern Ireland parties at Weston Park last summer.'*

Among other things his letter of appointment states:

> *'In the event that a public inquiry is recommended, the*

relevant government will implement that recommendation.'

He has recommended five inquiries – one in the Republic of Ireland (RoI) and four in Northern Ireland (NI) into the deaths of Pat Finucane, Rosemary Nelson, Robert Hamill and Billy Wright. The UK Government has agreed to the four inquiries, indeed those in relation to Rosemary Nelson and Robert Hamill have commenced, and the RoI Government has confirmed its acceptance of his recommendations. In NI this could lead to further investigations of, and files concerning police officers, either former or present, being referred to the Director of Public Prosecutions, which in turn could lead to cases.

In addition we have, thirdly, complaints to the Ombudsman in historical cases which could lead to further police investigations and police officers being charged.

If, as appears to be the case, the notion of a people at war has been accepted by Government and the prisoners of war released, should the slate be wiped clean for all, including police officers?

5. **Summary**

Together all of the above will create a situation of some complexity for this society, the Police Service of Northern Ireland and the Policing Board:

- An even more divided society than Northern Ireland has at present;
- The Chief Constable unable to deliver on his primary legislative role as a result of police time being consumed on investigations going back into the not so recent past;
- Investigations that are demanded in some quarters but that may not really address the needs of those who have suffered over the course of the Troubles;
- A deterioration in police morale;
- The financial implications of compensation cases against the Chief Constable;
- The financial implications of further inquiries consuming further resources which, if responsibility for Justice is devolved to Northern Ireland, could take from, for example, much needed health and education expenditures. Can this society afford financially to replicate the Bloody Sunday Inquiry?

6. **Options**

Bearing in mind the many differing perspectives, what are the options for a way forward?

Option 1: Article 2 of the ECHR states that '*everyone's right to life shall be protected by the law*'. Collusion and misdemeanours by the State must never happen and the perpetrators must be pursued through prosecution. Should the police, therefore, investigate all murders and measures to bring offenders to justice?

Option 2: Should we accept that in a war nasty things happen on both sides? If, as Sinn Fein has argued – and the argument appears to have been *implicitly* accepted – they were engaged in a war and not in terrorism, then should, as of, say, the signing of the Joint Declaration, the slate be wiped clean for all and should we as a society look to the future?

Or perhaps there is a middle option:

- Should the release of the prisoners be extended to an amnesty for all; and
- Should a Truth Commission led by a representative group of church leaders, mainly from Northern Ireland, be established to enable people to begin voluntarily to tell their stories (when the main paramilitary organisations agree to go to the Truth Commission, the United Kingdom Government could agree to do so too)?

7. **Action**

The undersigned believe that dealing with the issue of the past in Northern Ireland is critical to the future. We also believe that both the UK and RoI Governments have a duty to tackle this issue. We have a vested interest in them doing so – both because as members of this community we believe there is a societal cost of not dealing with it, but also because even with the extra investment in investigations we are concerned that the police service is being asked to deliver the impossible.

We have presented some thoughts and some options which are intended to be provocative. Only with provocative comments can this debate really get going. We urge both Governments to assume their rightful responsibility and start to help the Northern Ireland community to properly deal with our past.

8. **Way Forward**

This paper poses many questions but is not bold enough to suggest answers. That would only serve to disenfranchise the people of Northern Ireland who should rightfully have a say on how we hold the past in a healthy balance with the future. However, we do recommend that it is for the UK Government, in consultation with the RoI Government, to assume, and begin to discharge, their rightful duty, and to immediately establish a Cross Community Body which would:

- Deliberate on the past;
- Consult with the Northern Ireland community; and
- Make proposals to the UK Government as to a more constructive way forward in dealing with the past

We hope that the provocative questions and options set out in this paper will helpfully contribute to the work of that cross-community body.

Professor Sir Desmond Rea
Chairman

Mr Denis Bradley
Vice-Chairman

Hugh Orde
Chief Constable

June 2005

References:

'The Report Of The Independent Review Of Parades And Marches', 1997
'A New Beginning: Policing In Northern Ireland,' The Report Of The Independent Commission On Policing For Northern Ireland, September 1999
'Statement By The Police Ombudsman For Northern Ireland On Her Investigation Into Matters Relating To The Omagh Bombing On August 15 1998', 12 December 2001
'Seeking To Hold The Past In Healthy Balance With The Future', Desmond Rea and Denis Bradley, 2003
'Cory Collusion Inquiry Reports', Judge Peter Cory 2003 and 2004
'Ways Of Dealing With Northern Ireland's Past: Interim Report – Victims And Survivors', the Northern Ireland Affairs Committee, 8 April 2005
'War Is Easy To Declare, Peace Is An Elusive Prize', Hugh Orde at the Trinity College Colloquium, 10 June 2005
Irish Times, Dan Keenan, 14 October 2005
'Policing The Past To Police The Future', Hugh Orde at Queen's University, 13 November 2006
'Can The Past Be Policed? Lessons from the Historical Enquiries Team, Northern Ireland,' Dr Patricia Lundy, Law and Social Challenges, Volume 11, 2009
'The Report Of The Consultative Group On The Past', 23 January, 2009
'Report Of The Bloody Sunday Inquiry', Lord Saville, 15 June, 2010
The Financial Times, John Lloyd, 16 June 2010
The Economist, June 2010
Northern Ireland Since 1969, Paul Dixon and Eamonn O'Kane, Pearson Education Ltd, Harlow, 2011
Irish Times, Mark Heaney, 23 February 2013
Irish Times, 21 March 2013
The Belfast Telegraph, 17 April 2013
'Together, Building A United Community', Northern Ireland Executive May 2013
'Inspection Of The Police Service Of Northern Ireland Historical Enquiries Team', Her Majesty's Inspectorate of Constabulary, 3 July 2013

Index